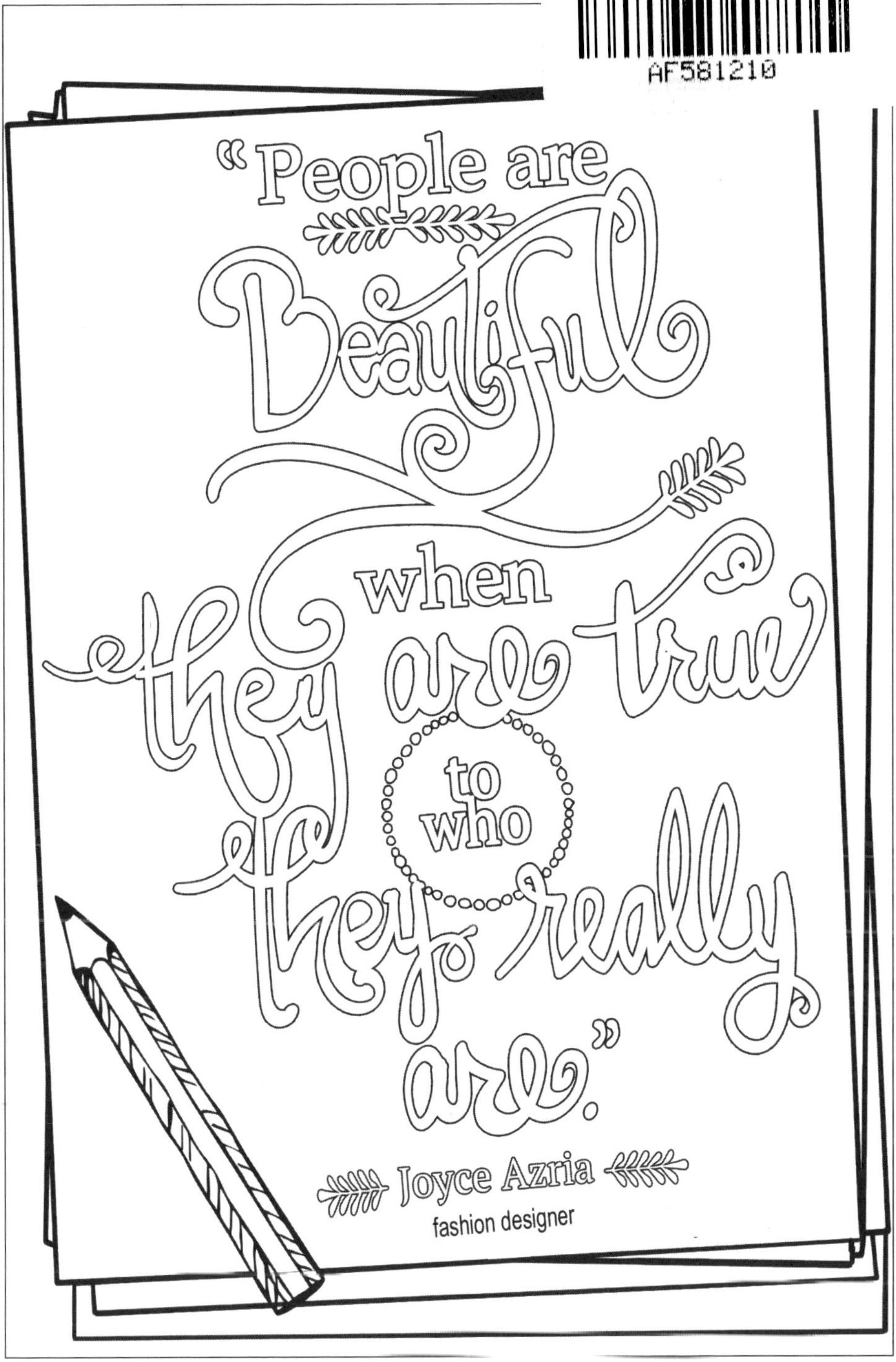

"People are Beautiful when they are true to who they really are."

Joyce Azria
fashion designer

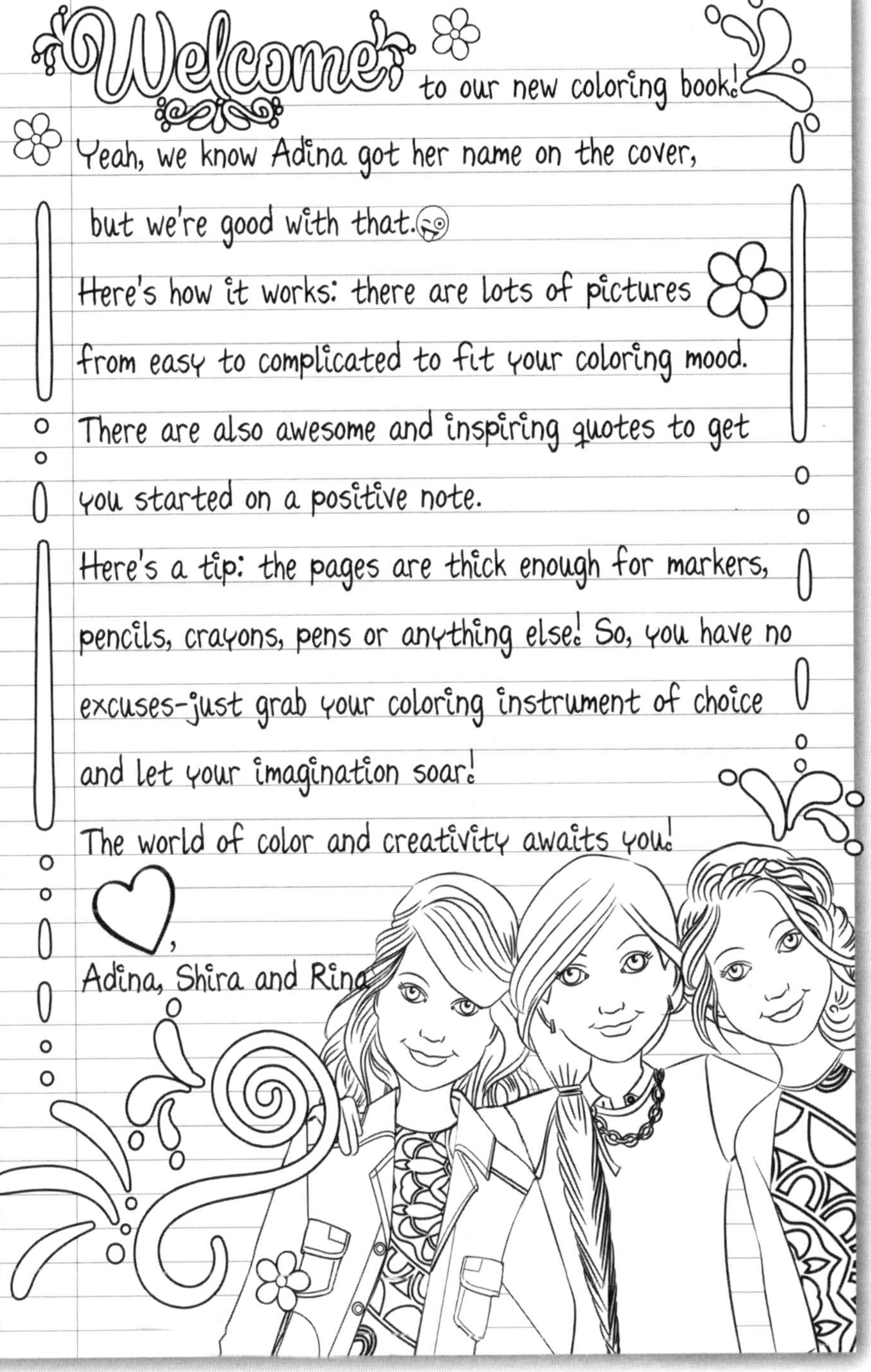

Welcome to our new coloring book!

Yeah, we know Adina got her name on the cover, but we're good with that.

Here's how it works: there are lots of pictures from easy to complicated to fit your coloring mood. There are also awesome and inspiring quotes to get you started on a positive note.

Here's a tip: the pages are thick enough for markers, pencils, crayons, pens or anything else! So, you have no excuses-just grab your coloring instrument of choice and let your imagination soar!

The world of color and creativity awaits you!

♥,

Adina, Shira and Rina

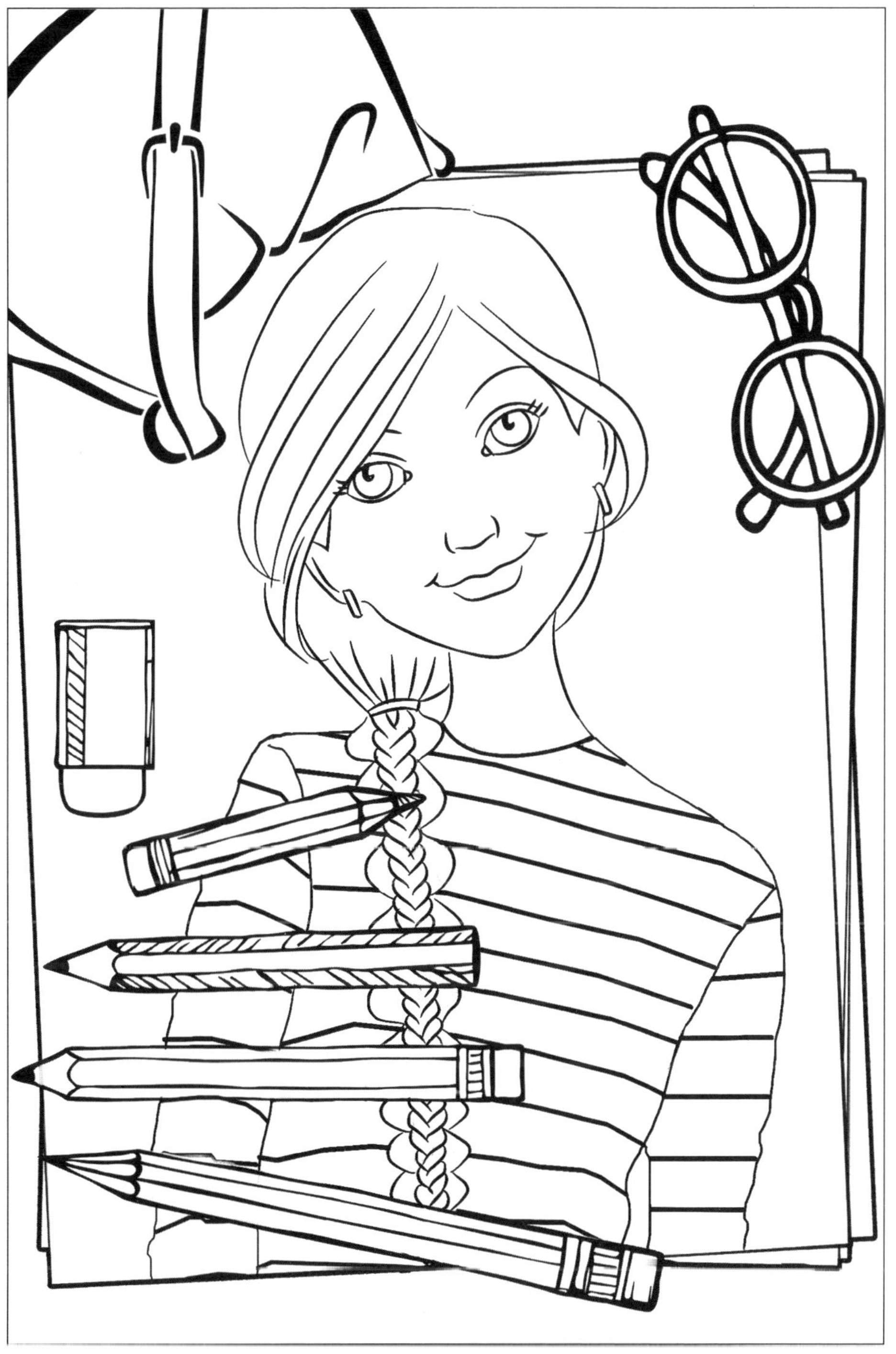

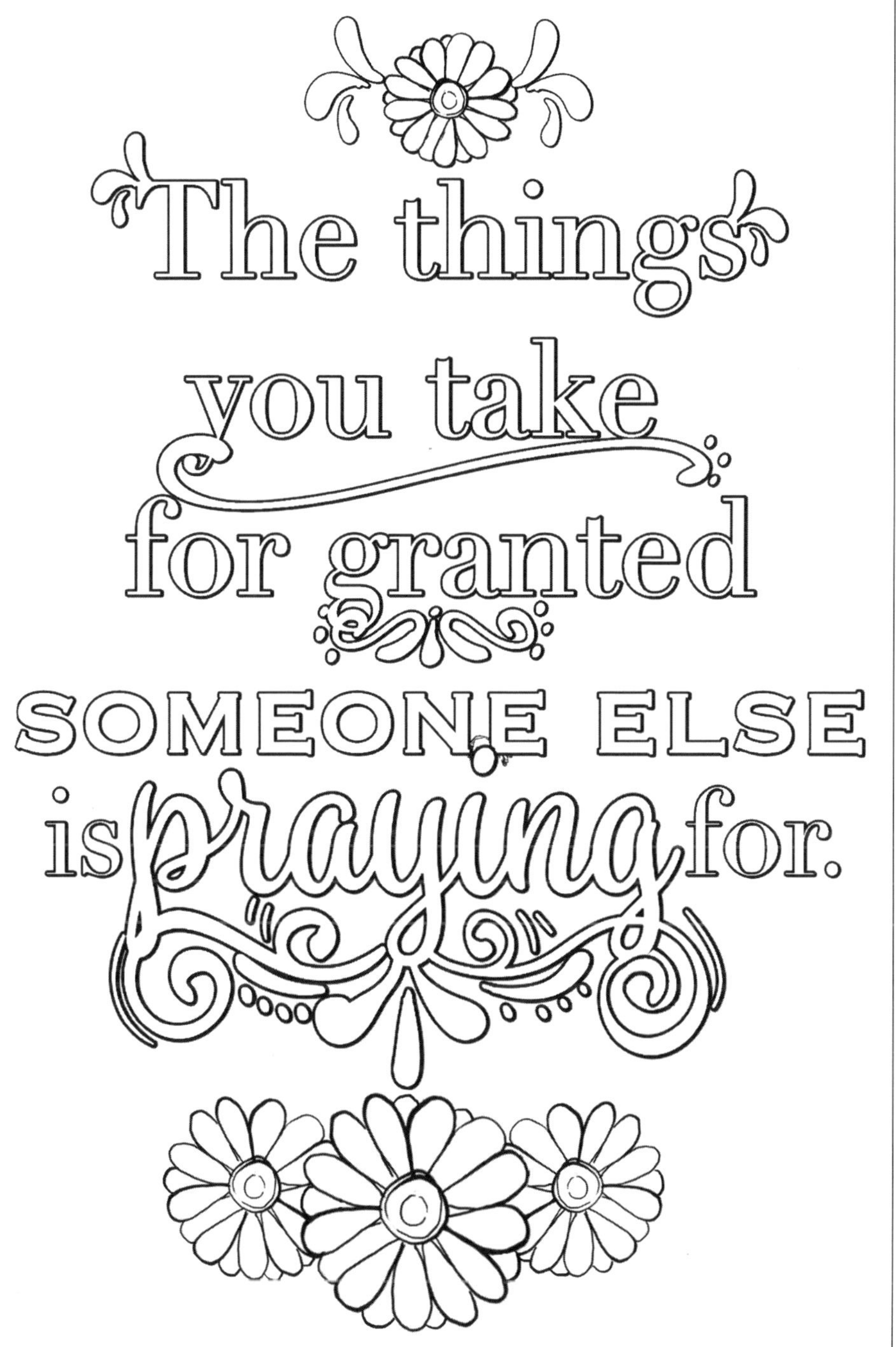
The things
you take
for granted
SOMEONE ELSE
is praying for.

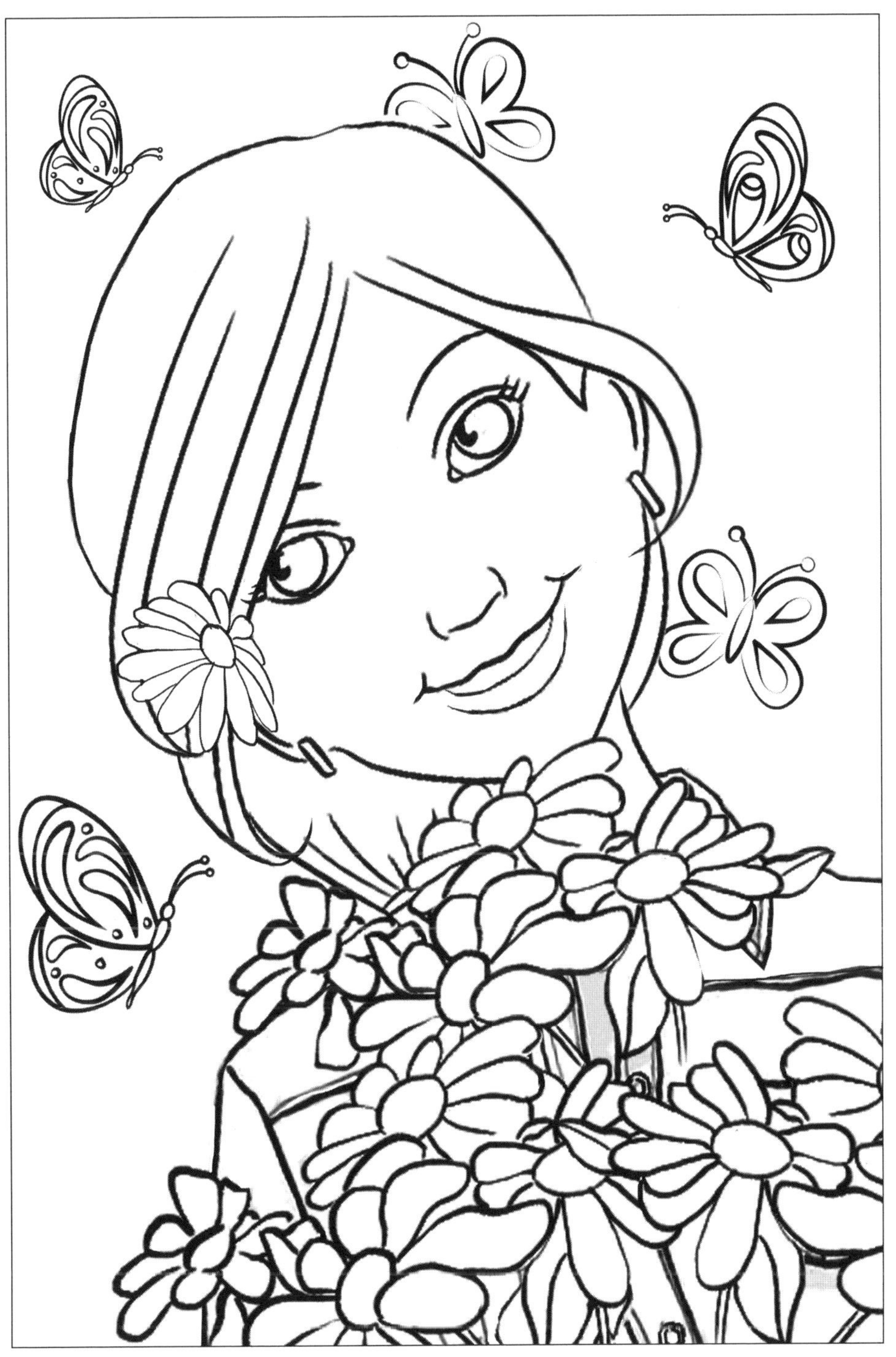

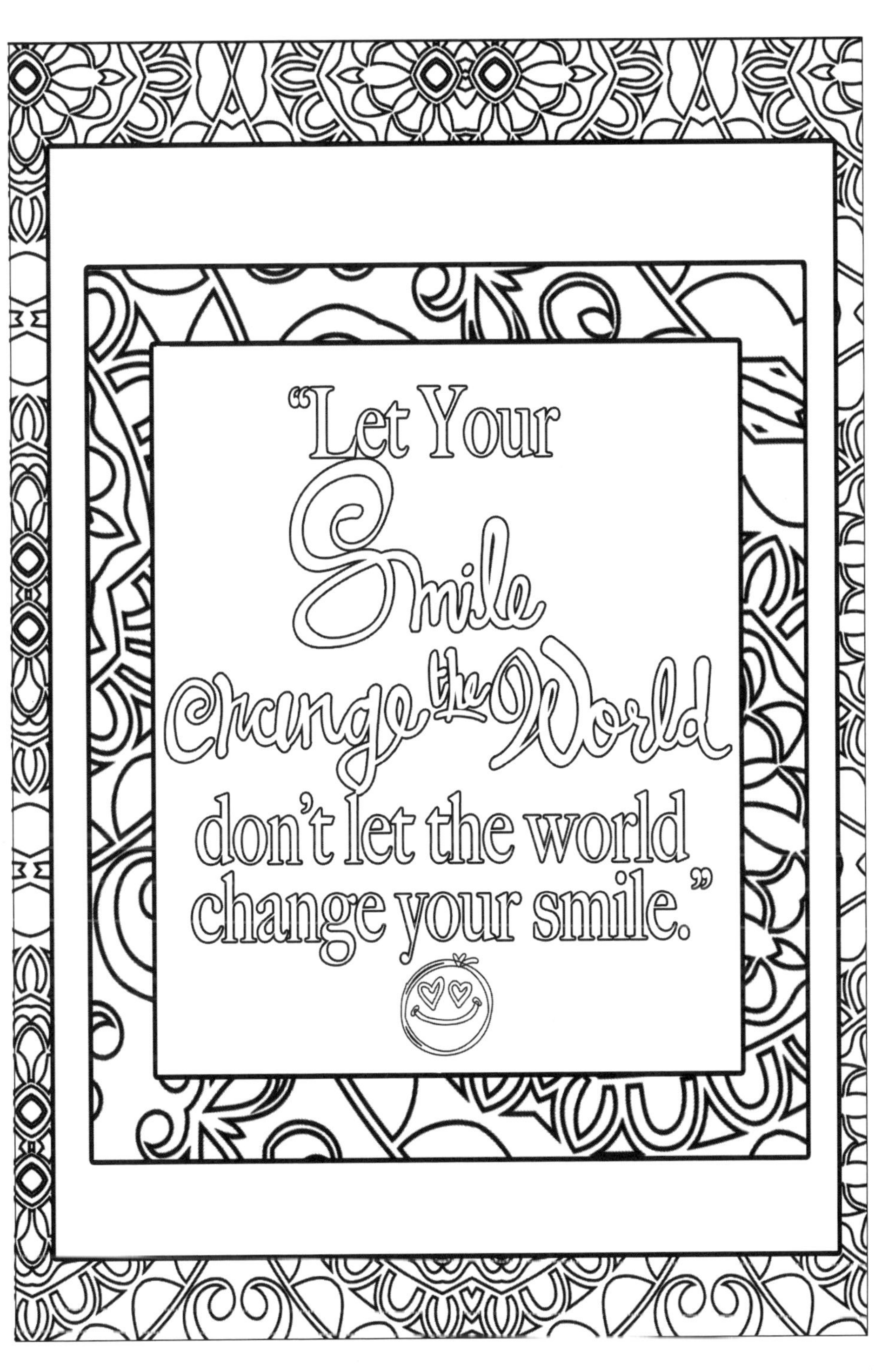
"Let Your
Smile
Change the World
don't let the world
change your smile."

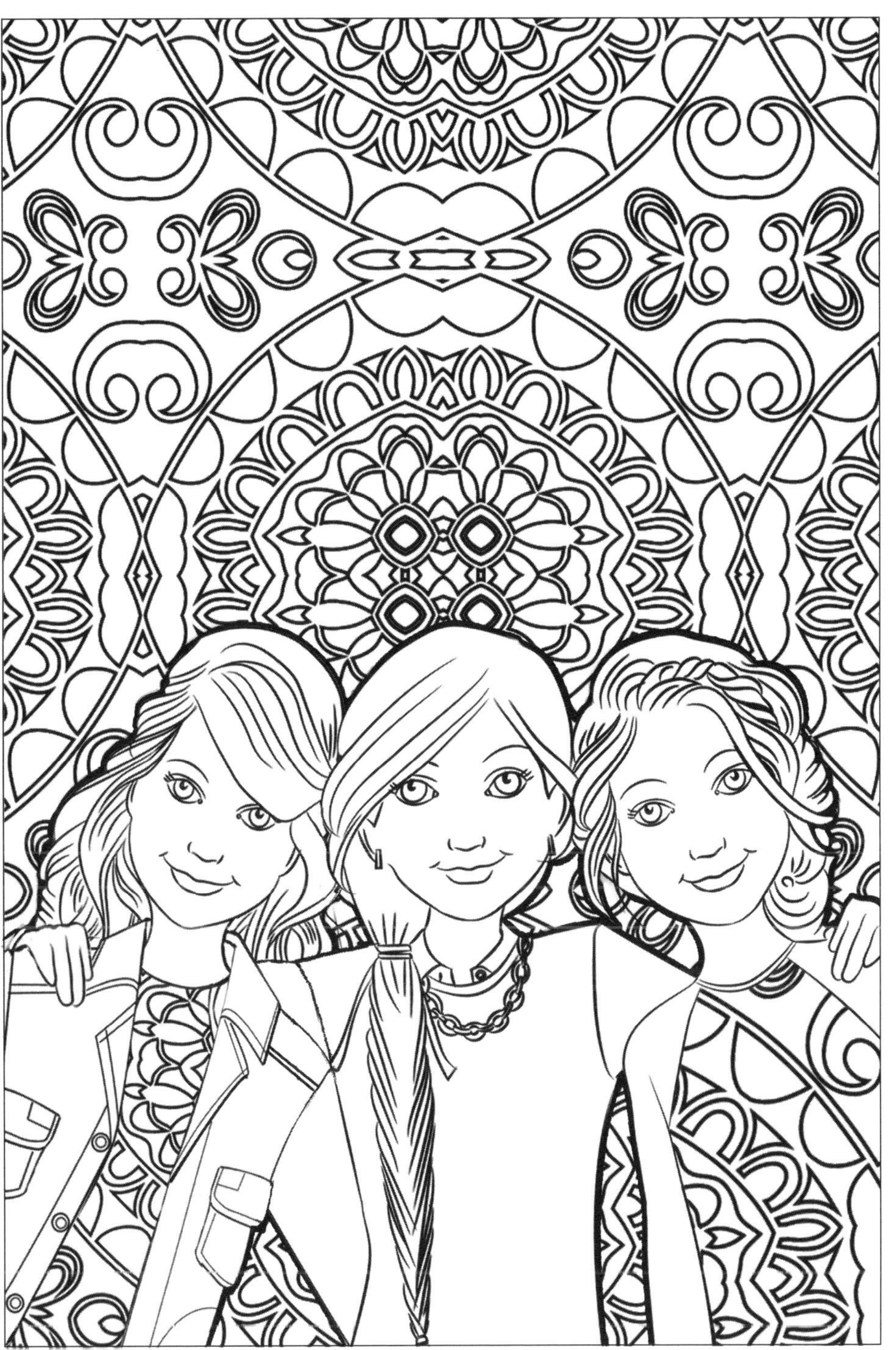

You were born to bring something to the world that no one else can!

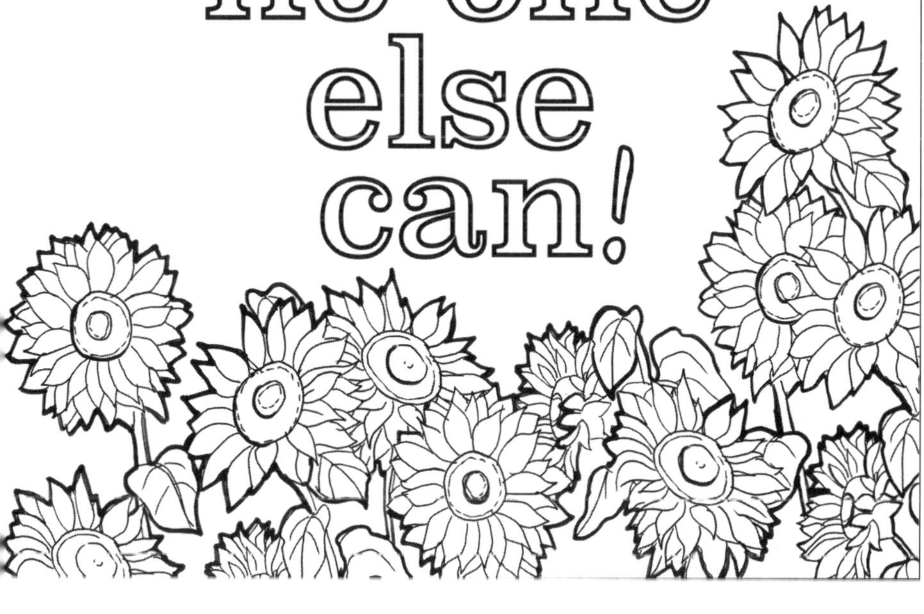

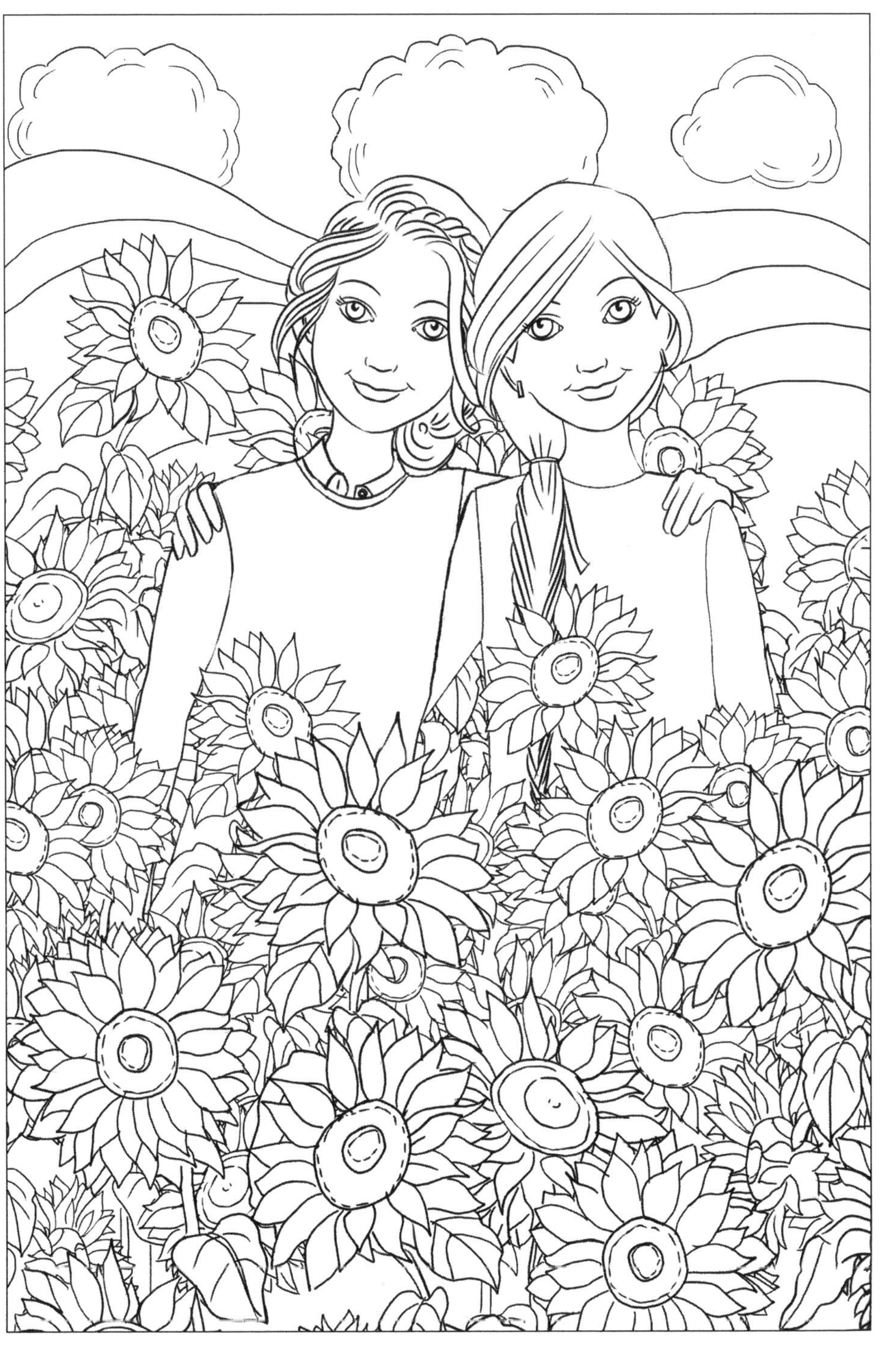

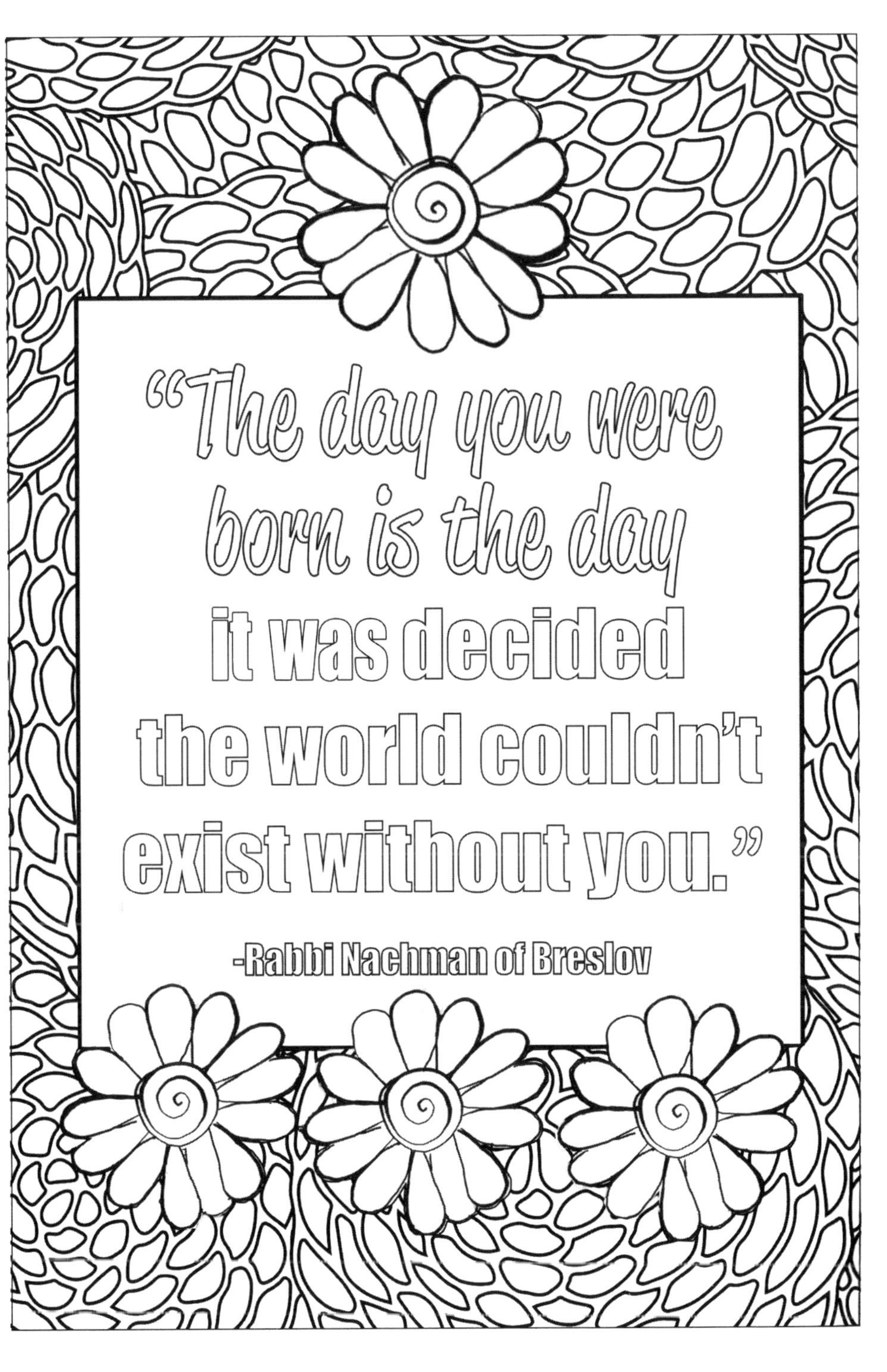
"The day you were born is the day it was decided the world couldn't exist without you."
-Rabbi Nachman of Breslov

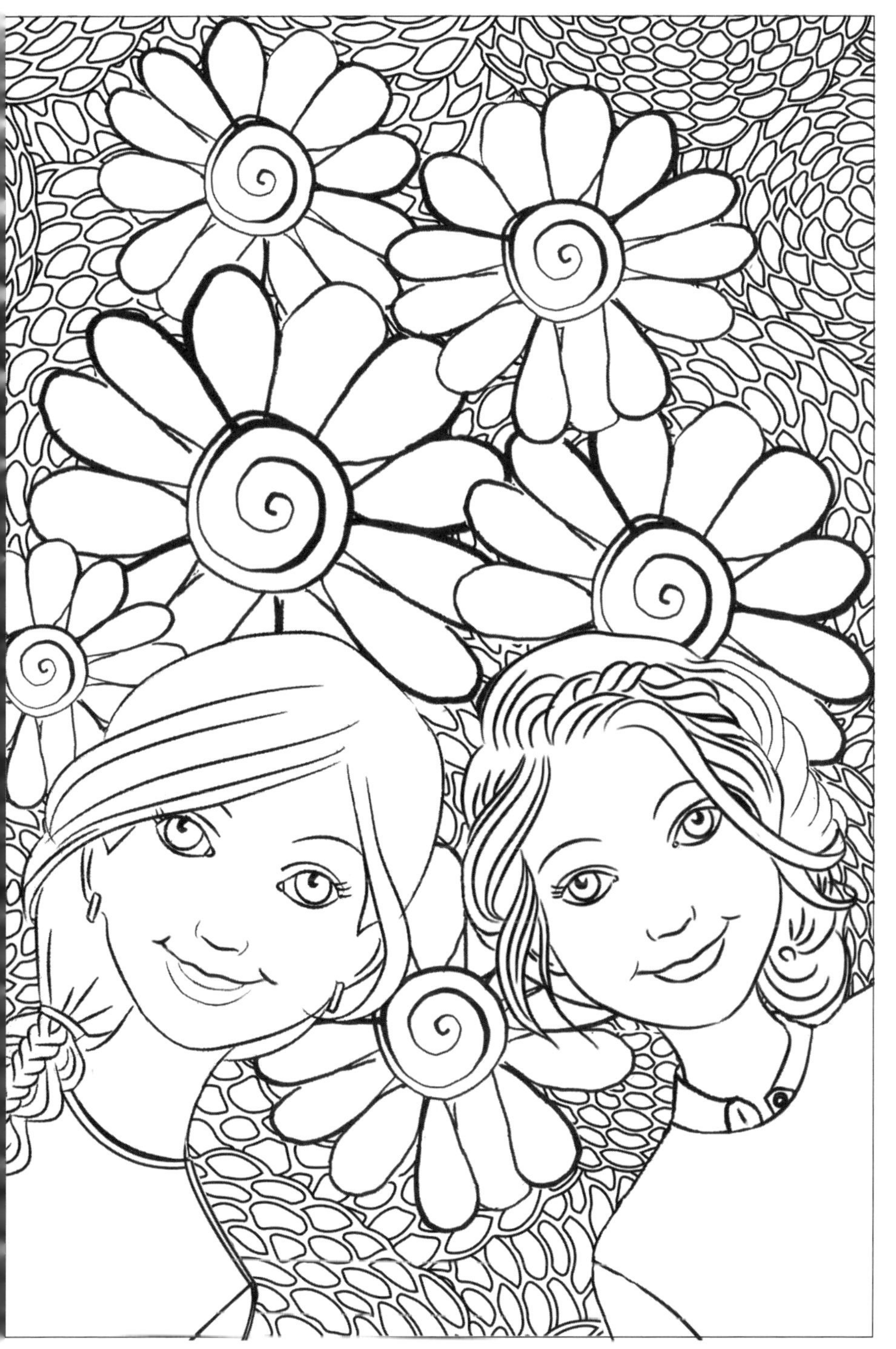

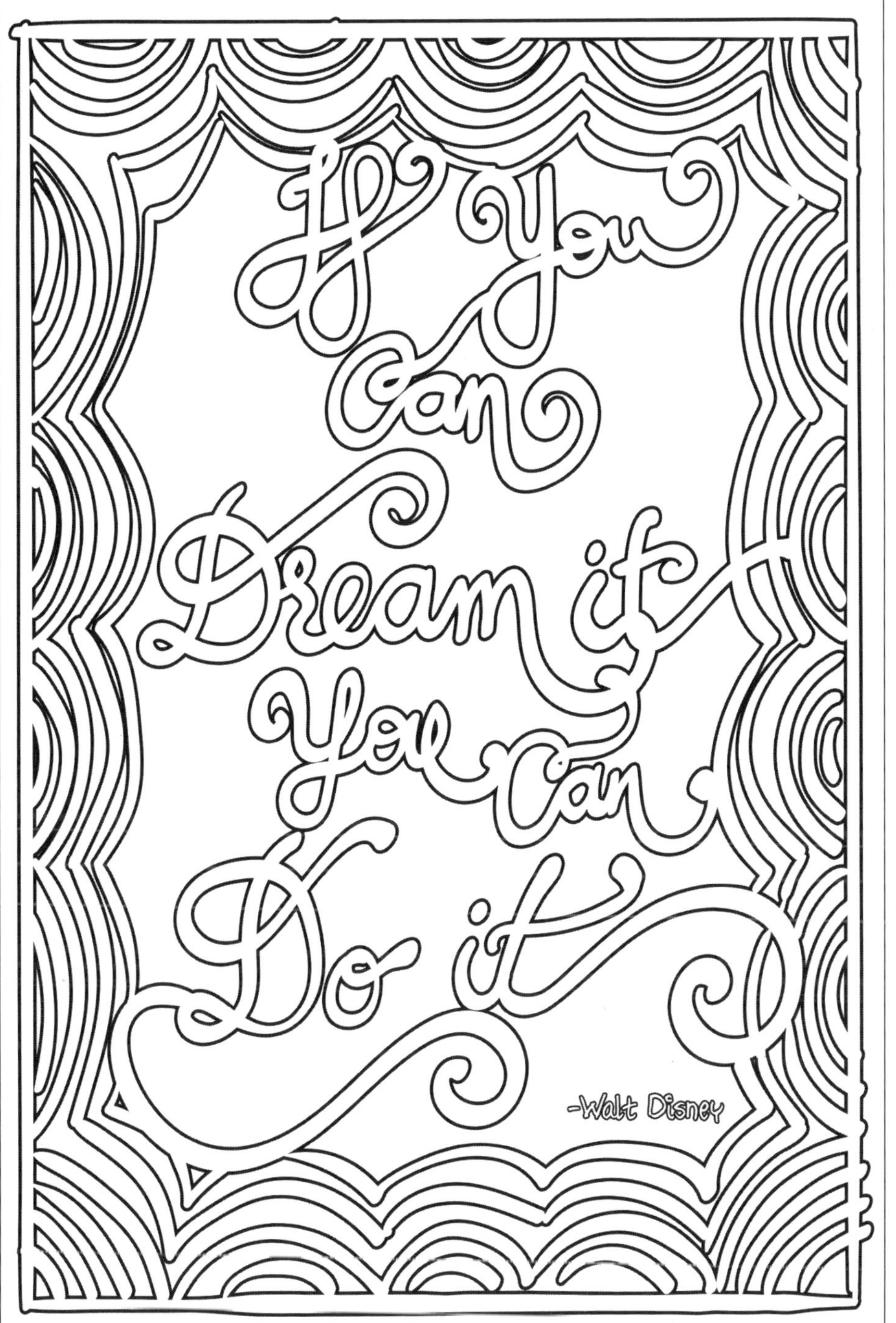
If You Can Dream it You Can Do it
-Walt Disney

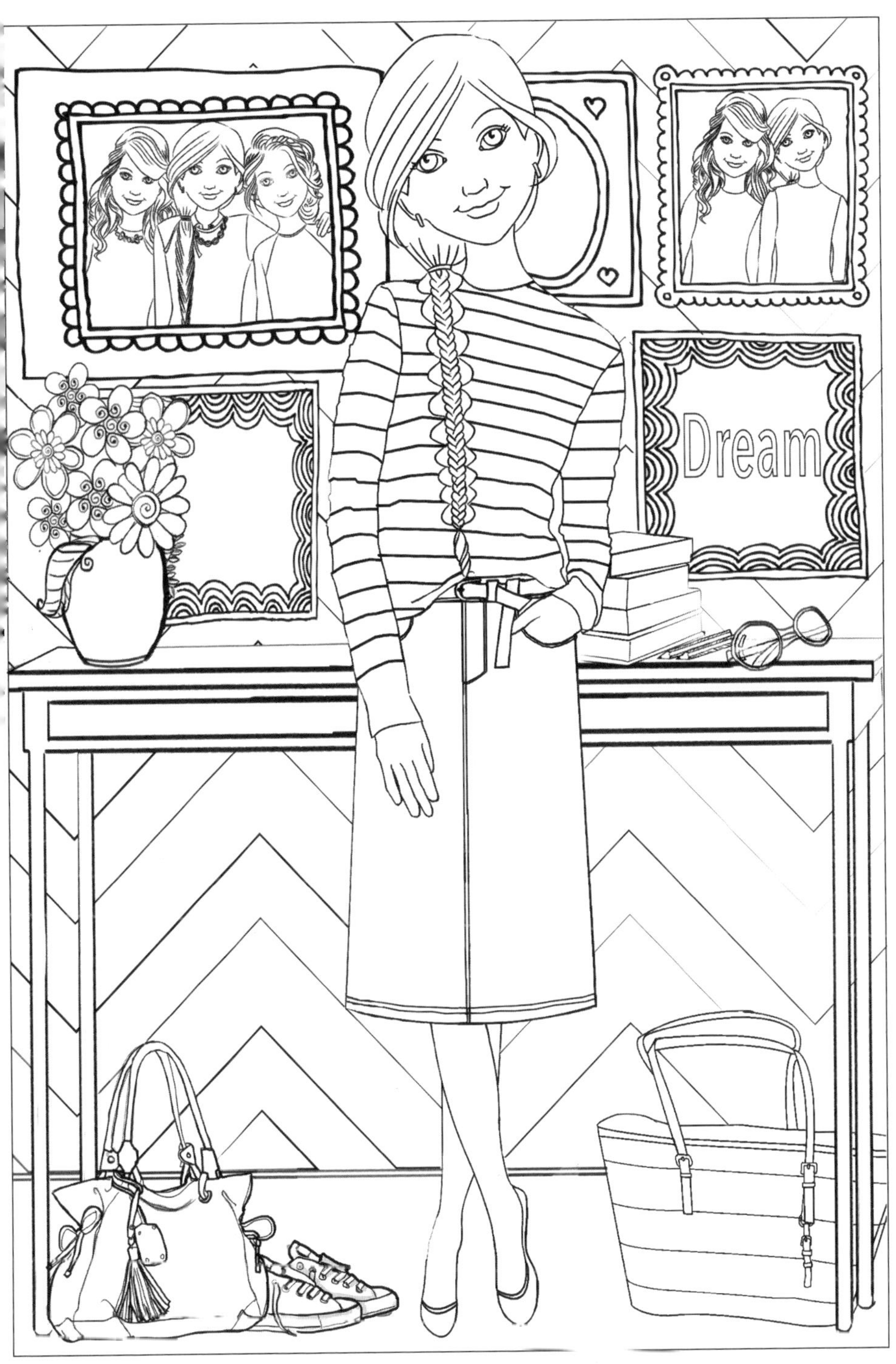
Dream

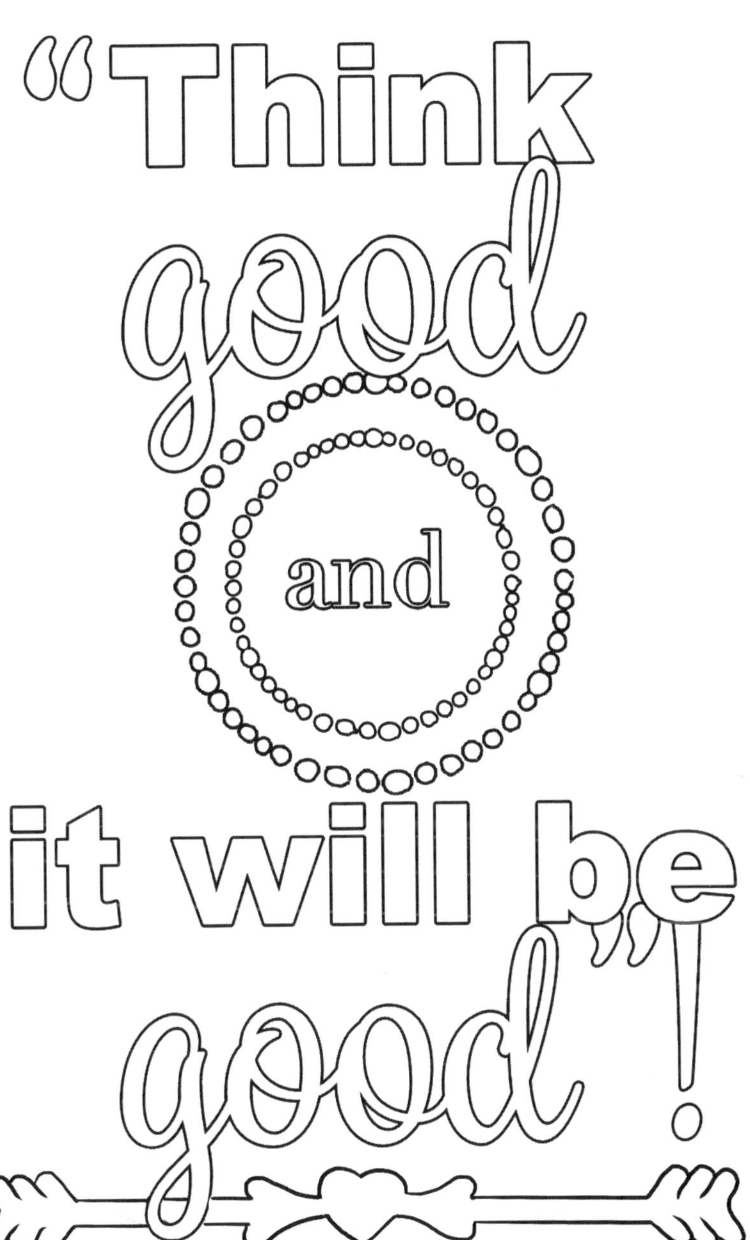

Rabbi Menachem Mendel of Lubavitch

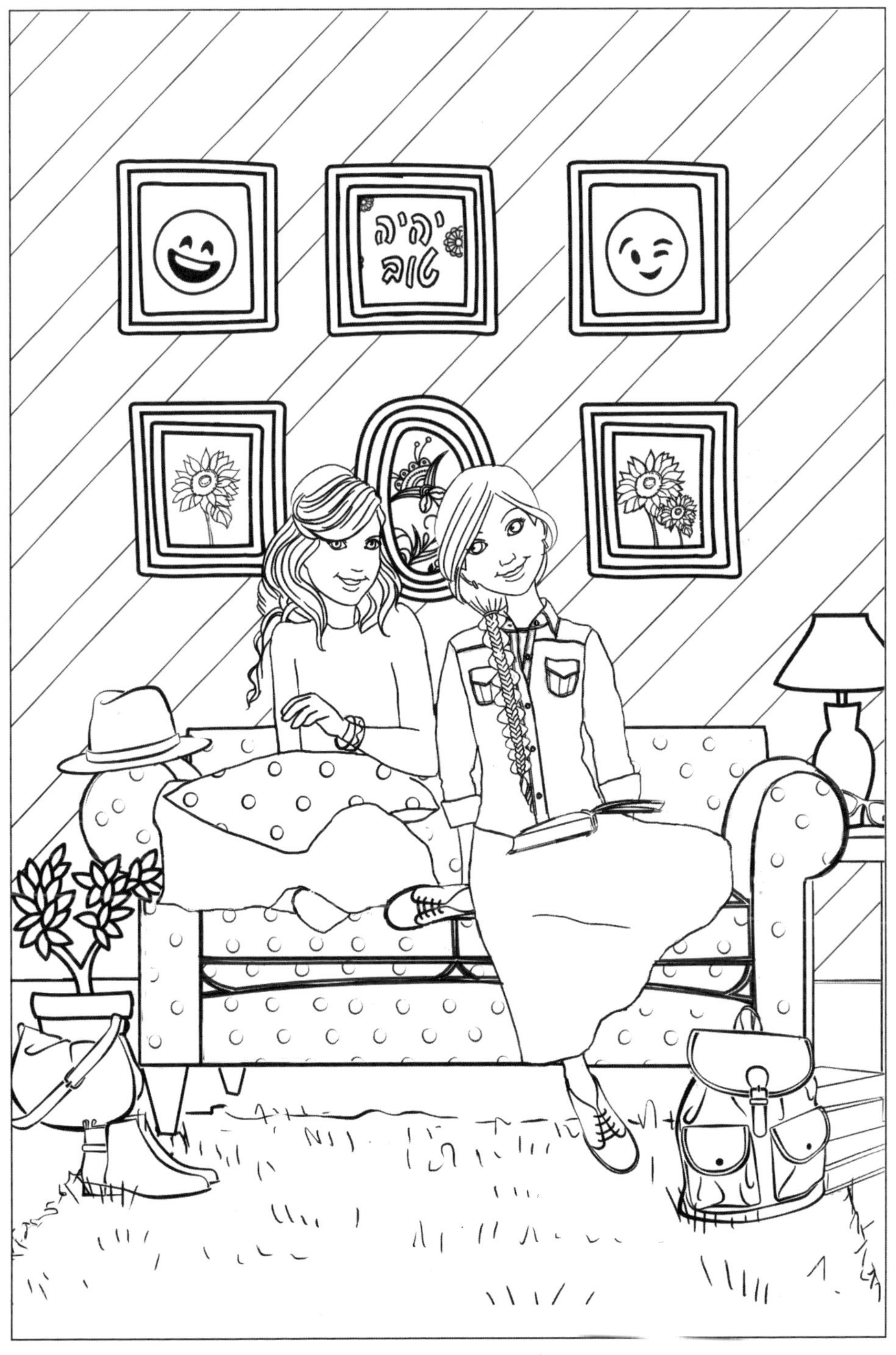
יהיה
טוב

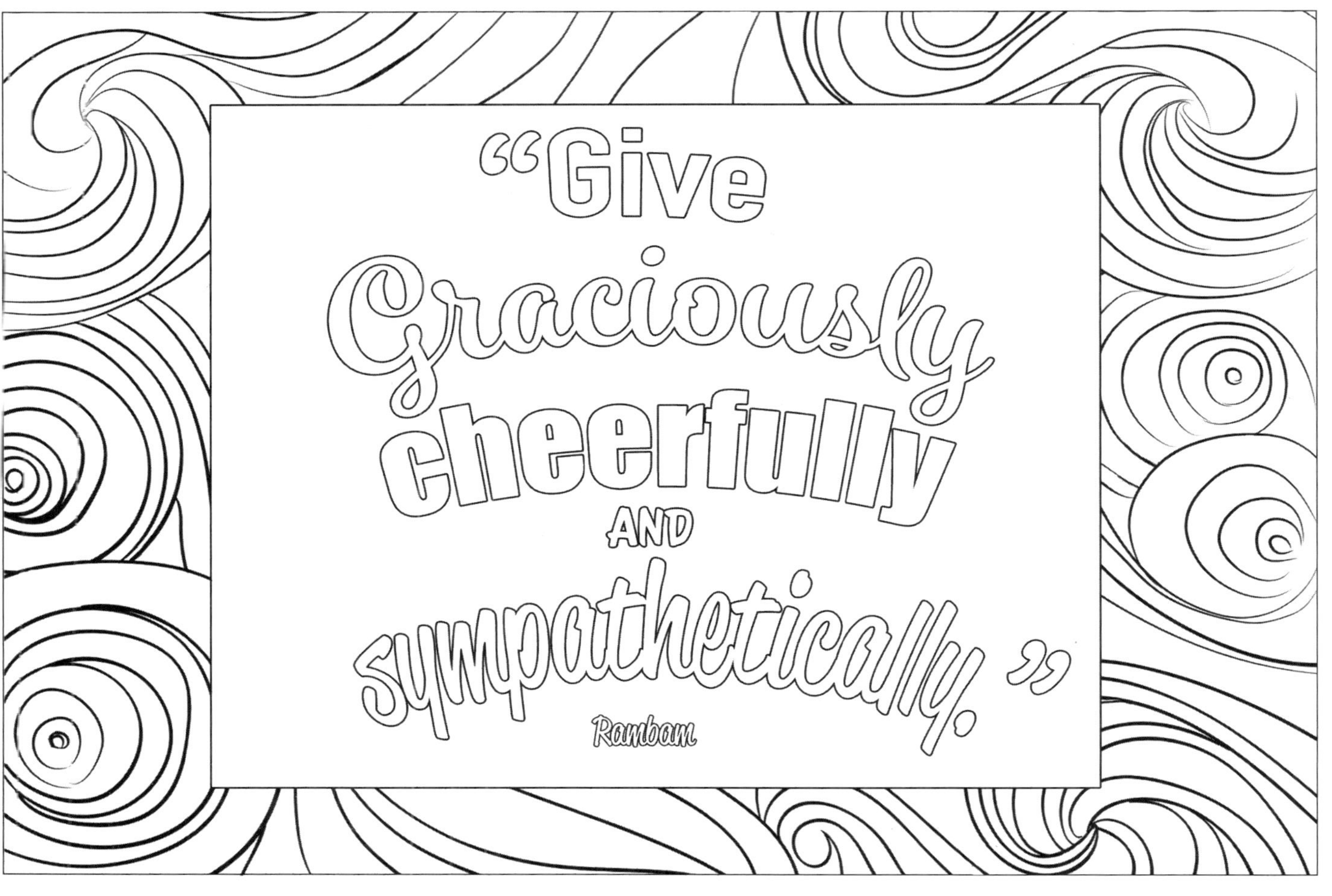
"Give
Graciously
cheerfully
AND
sympathetically."
Rambam

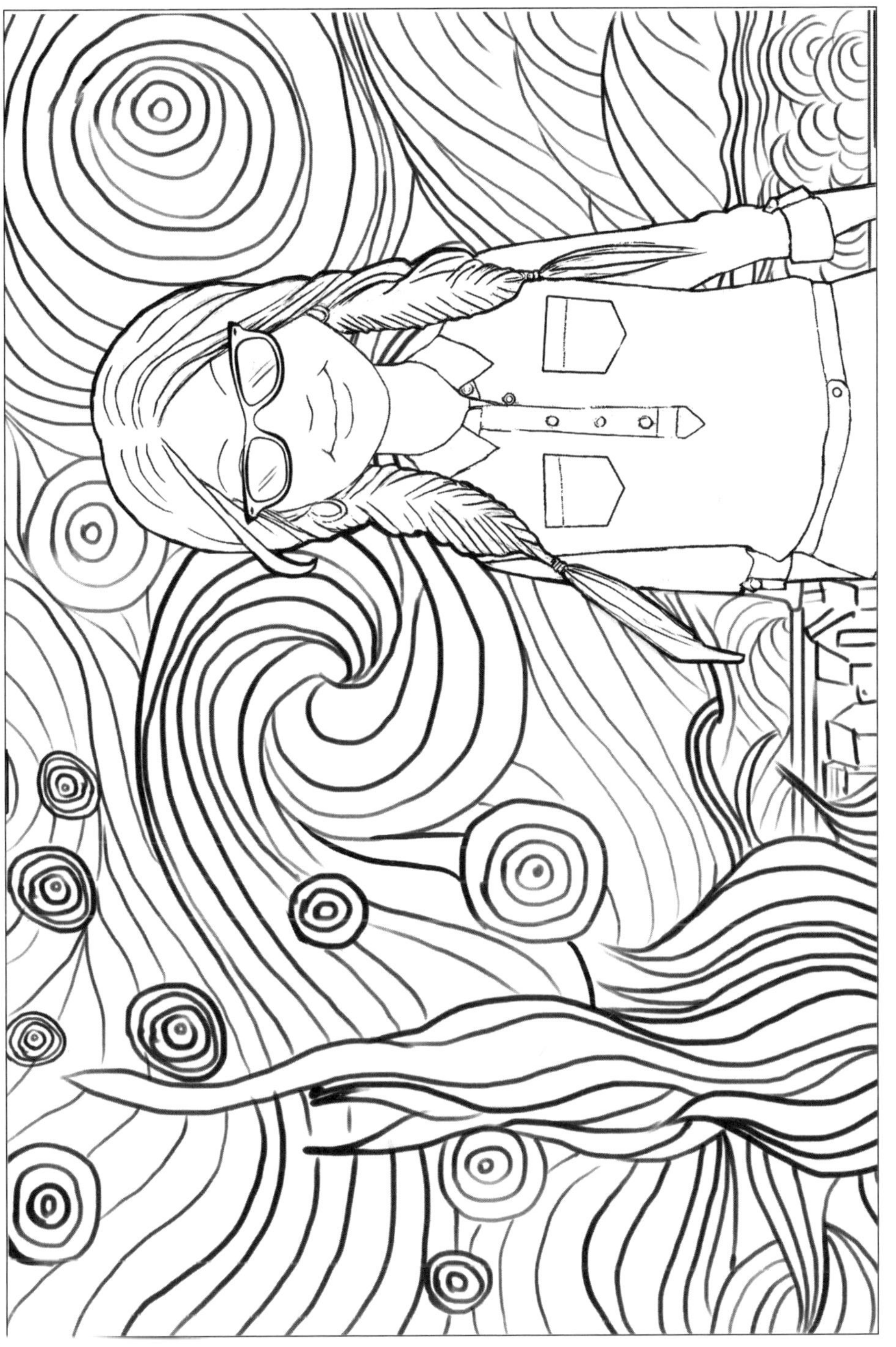

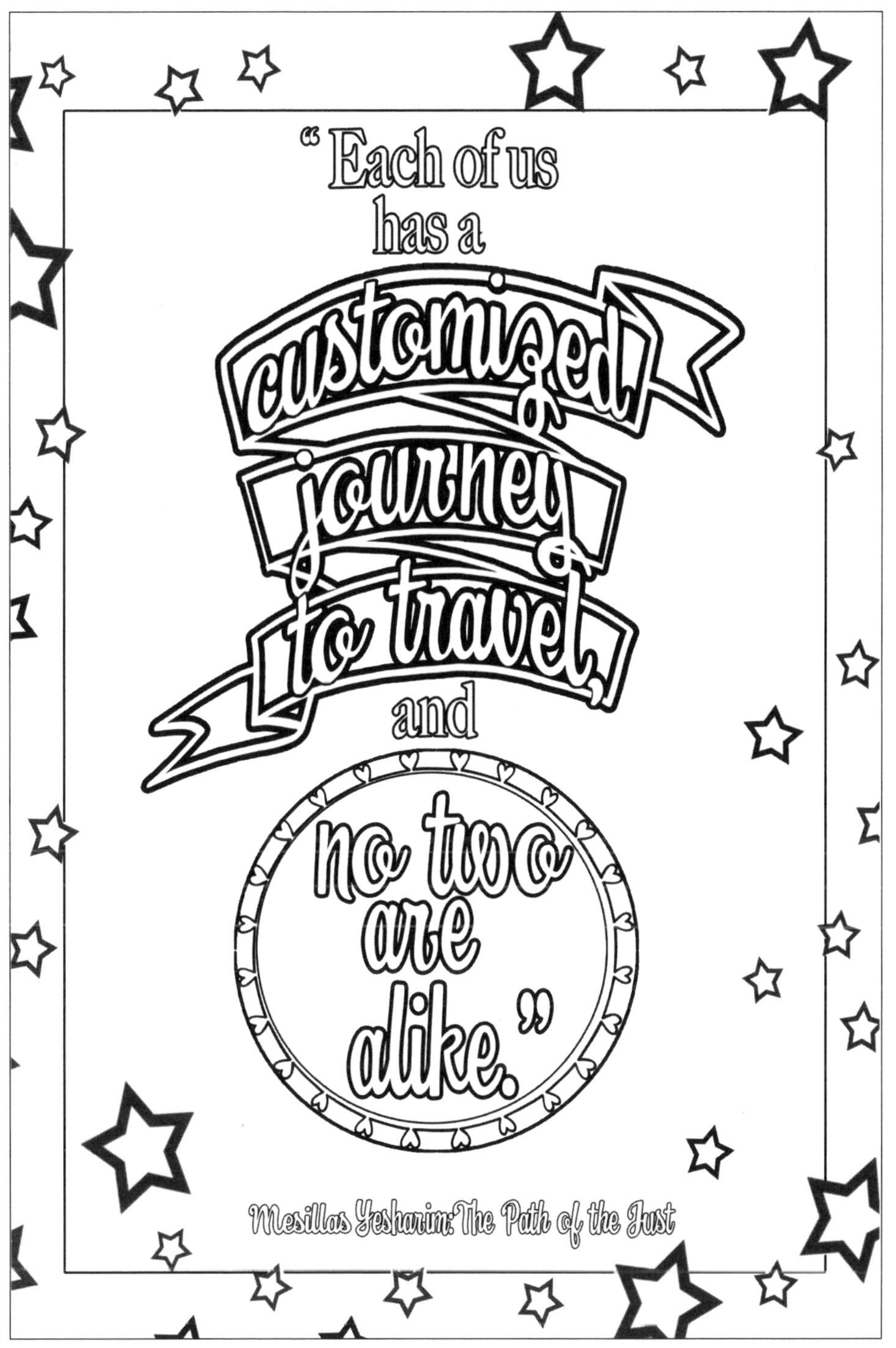
" Each of us
has a
customized
journey
to travel,
and
no two
are
alike."
Mesillas Yesharim: The Path of the Just

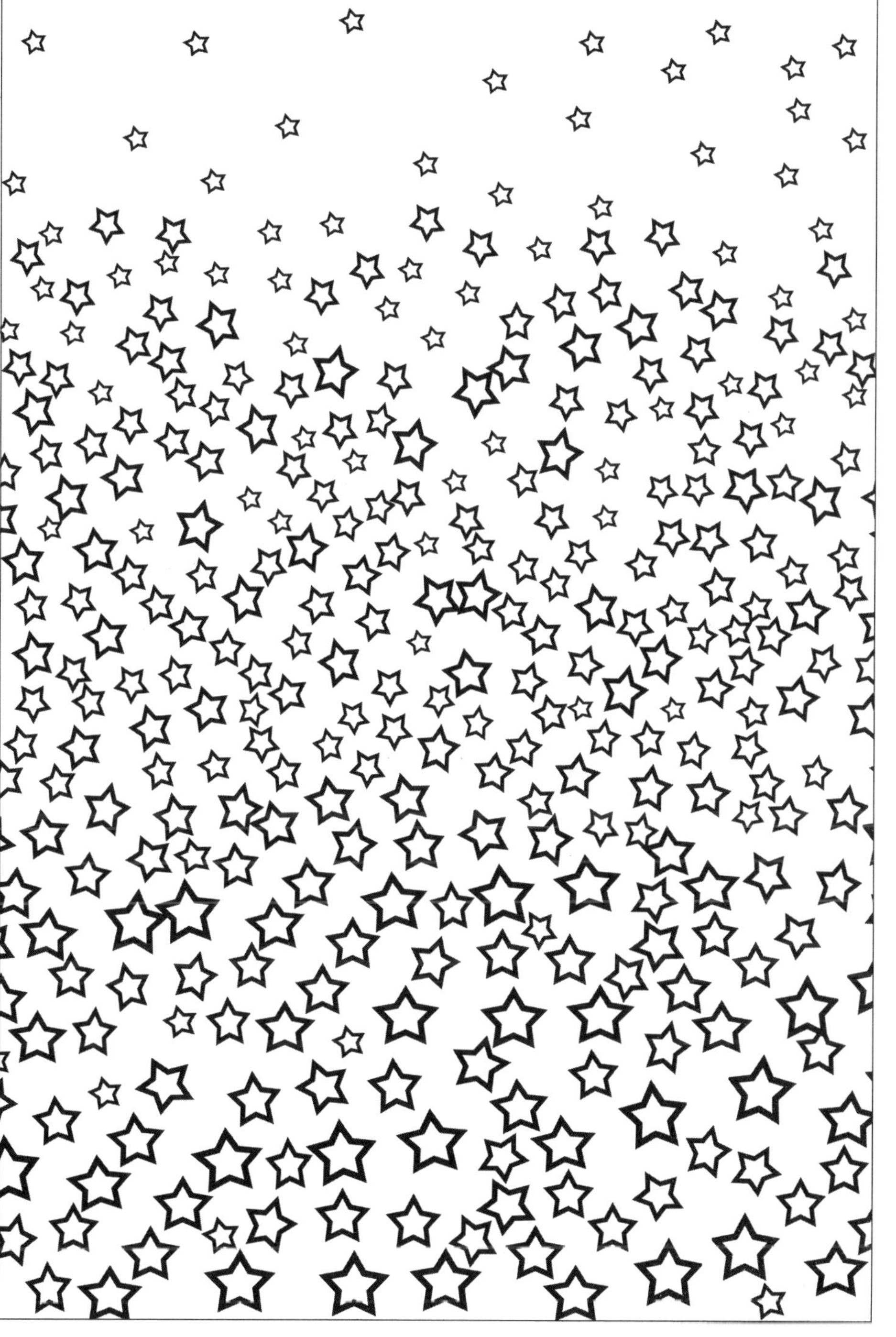

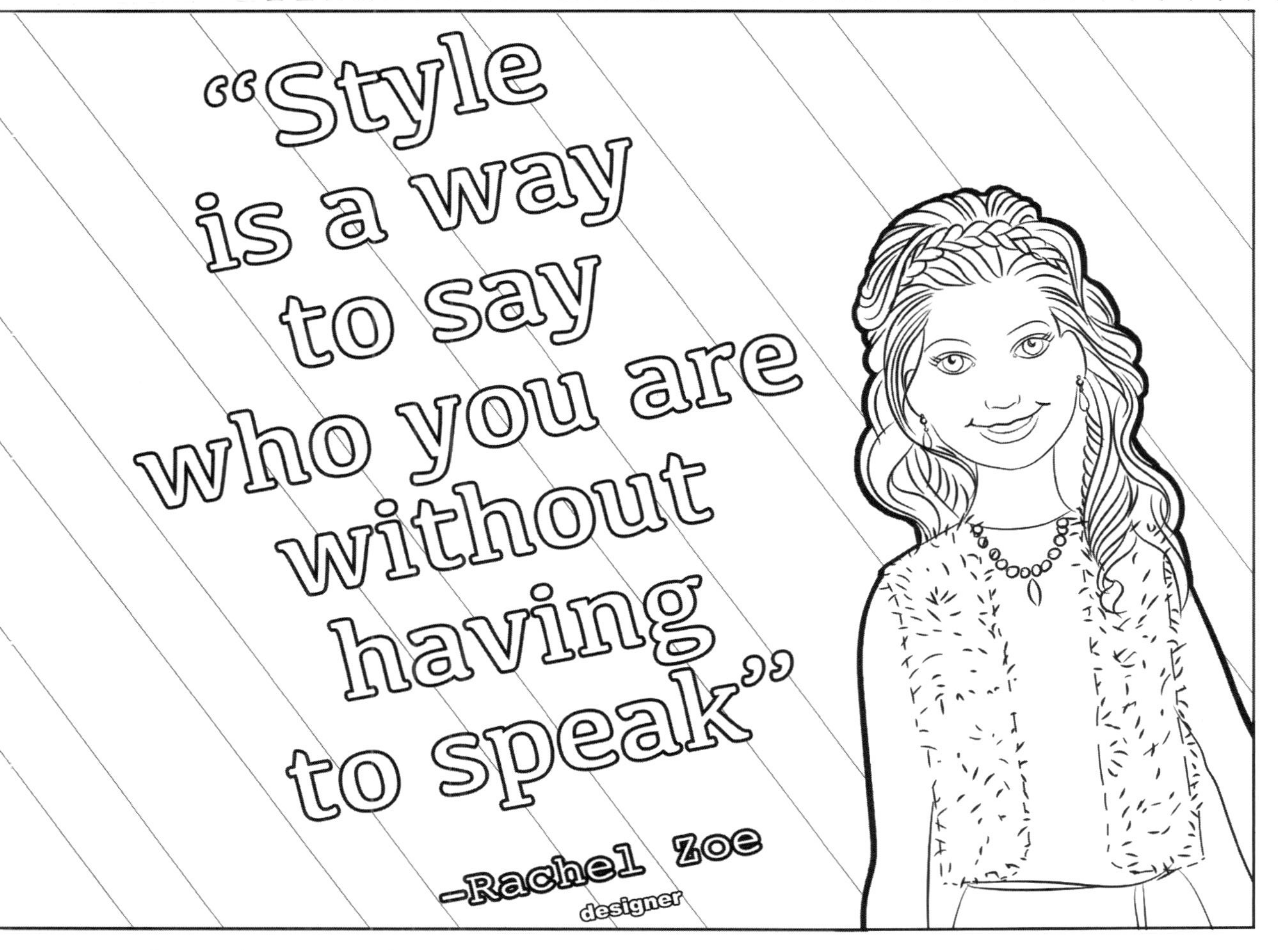
"Style
is a way
to say
who you are
without
having
to speak"
–Rachel Zoe
designer

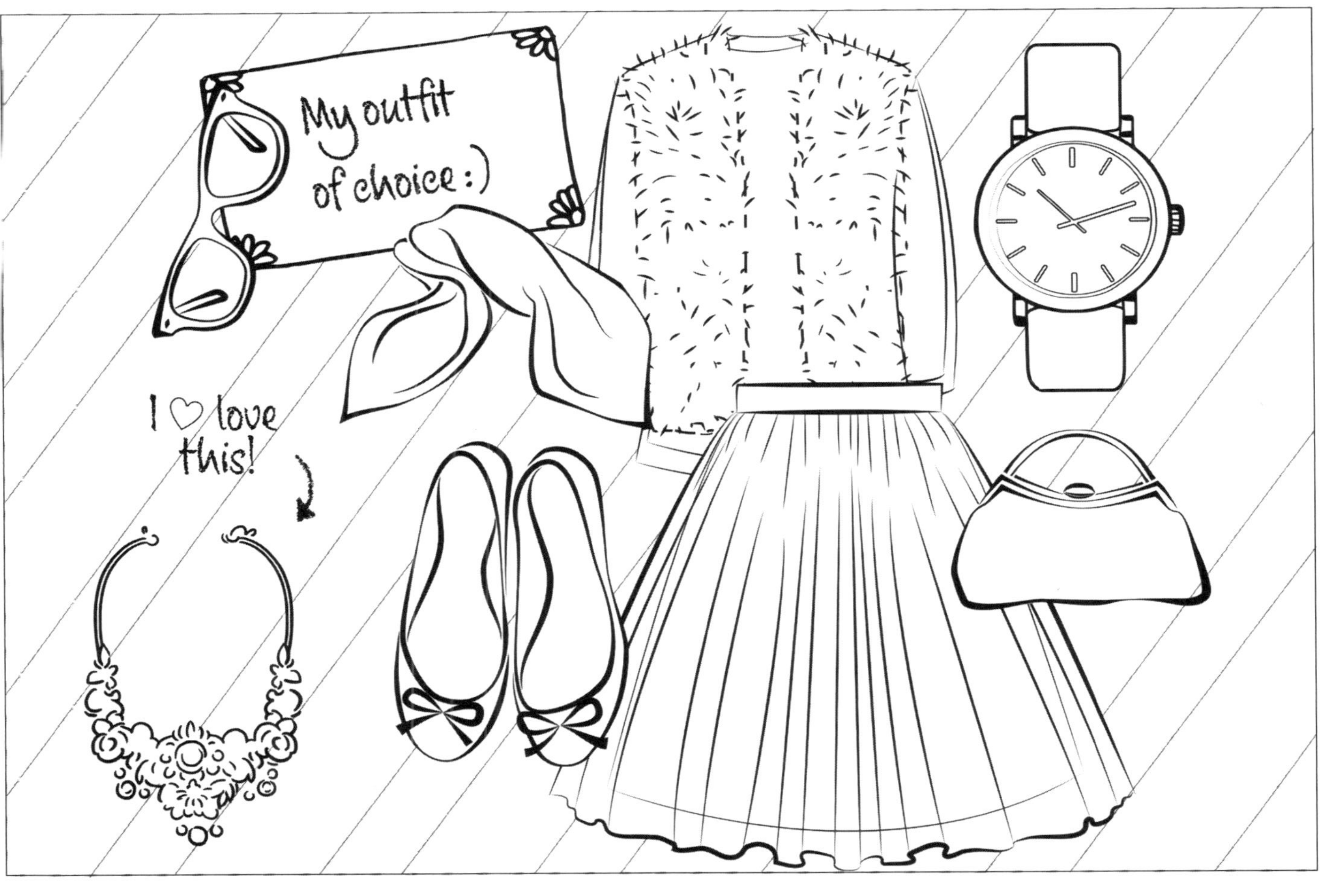
My outfit
of choice :)
I ♡ love
this!

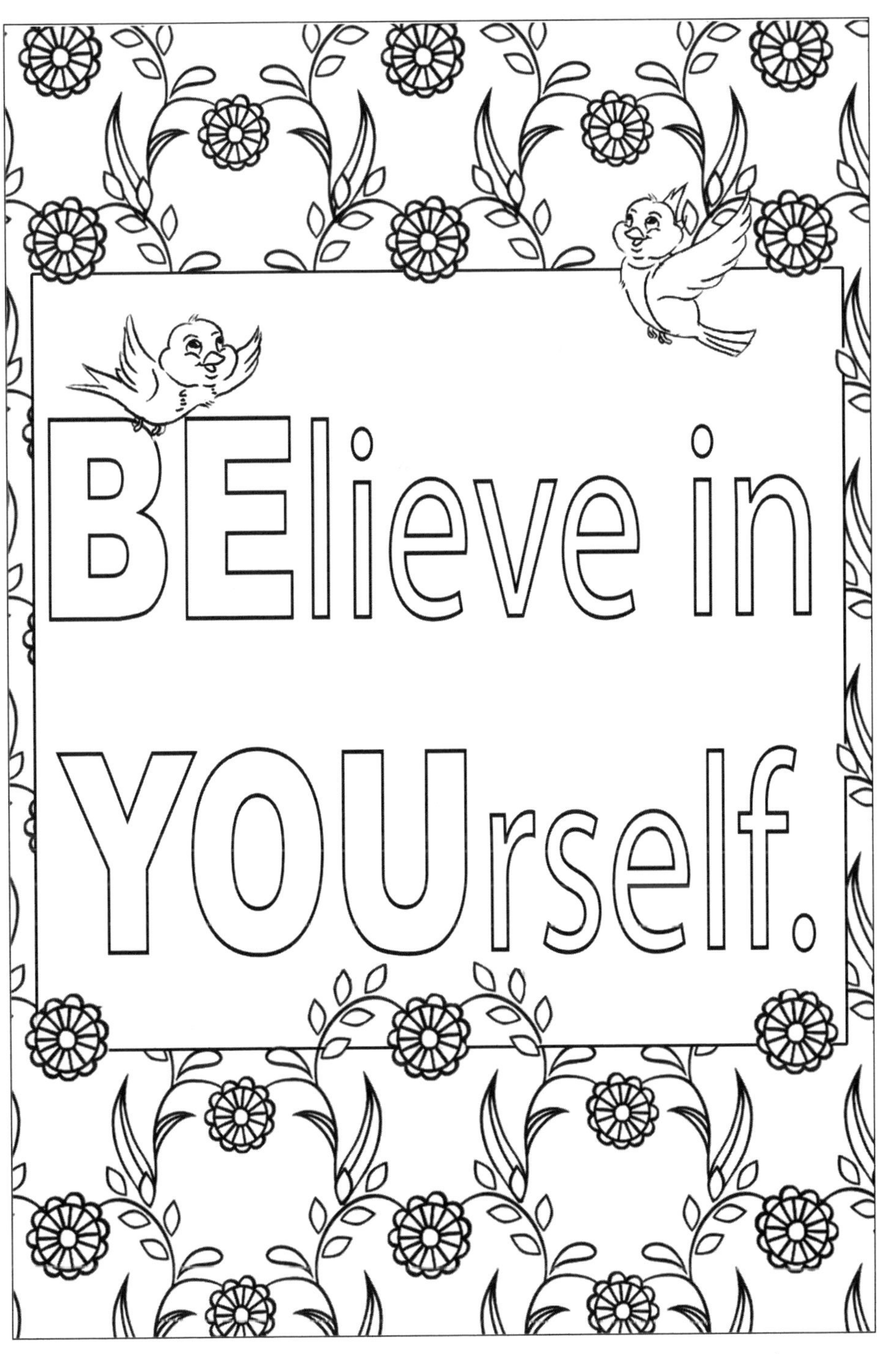
BElieve in
YOUrself.

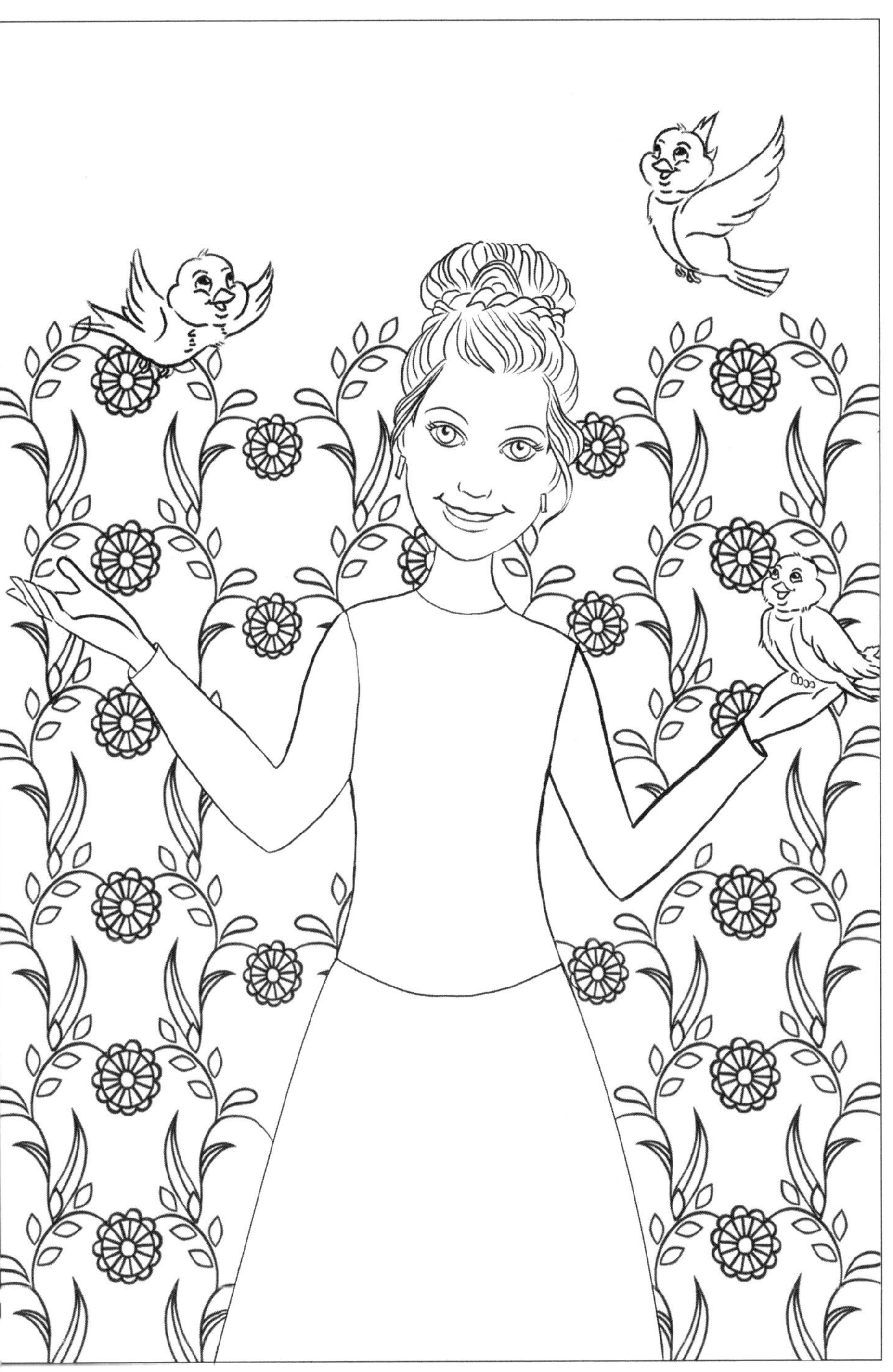

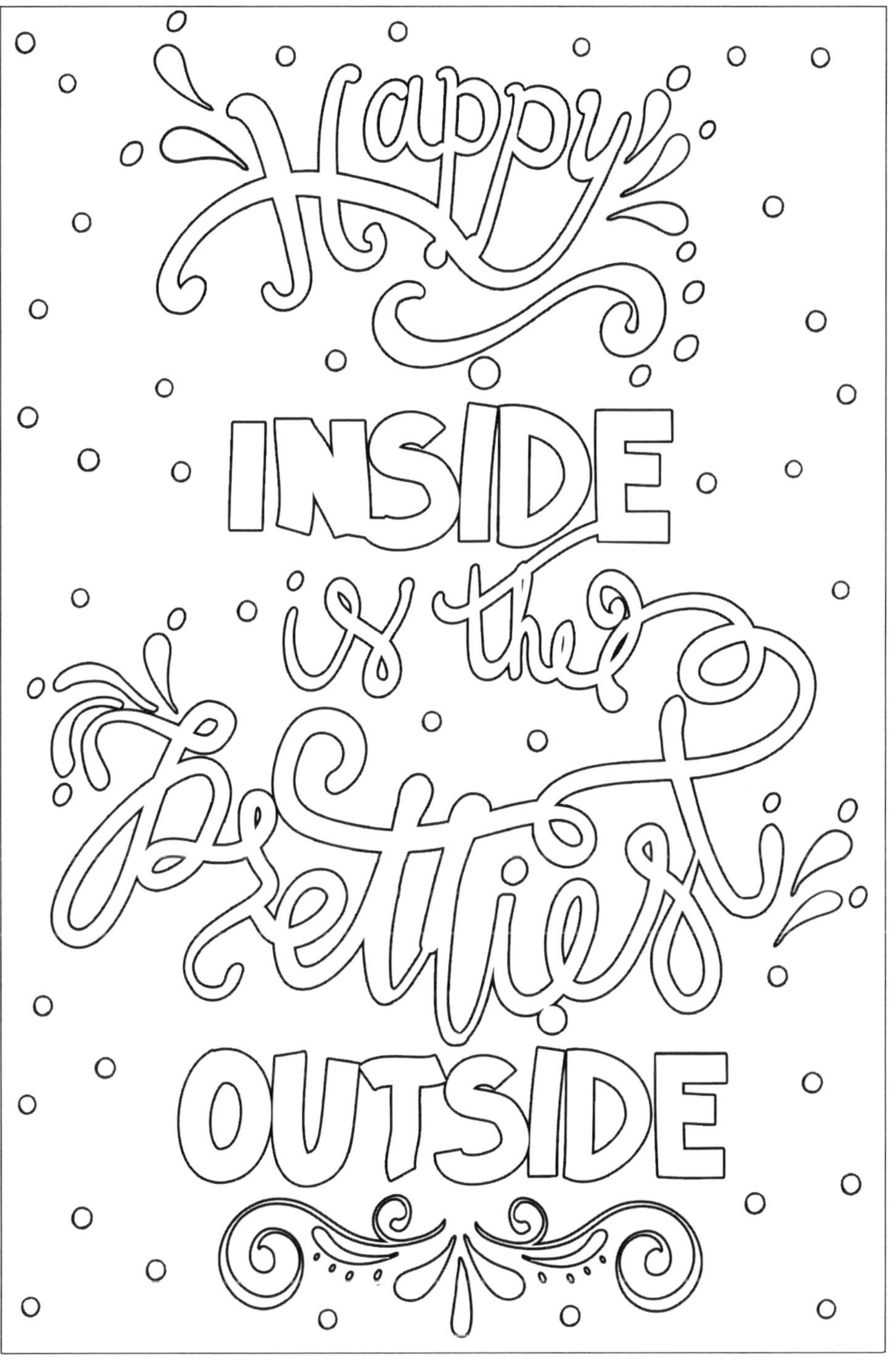
Happy
INSIDE
is the
Prettiest
OUTSIDE

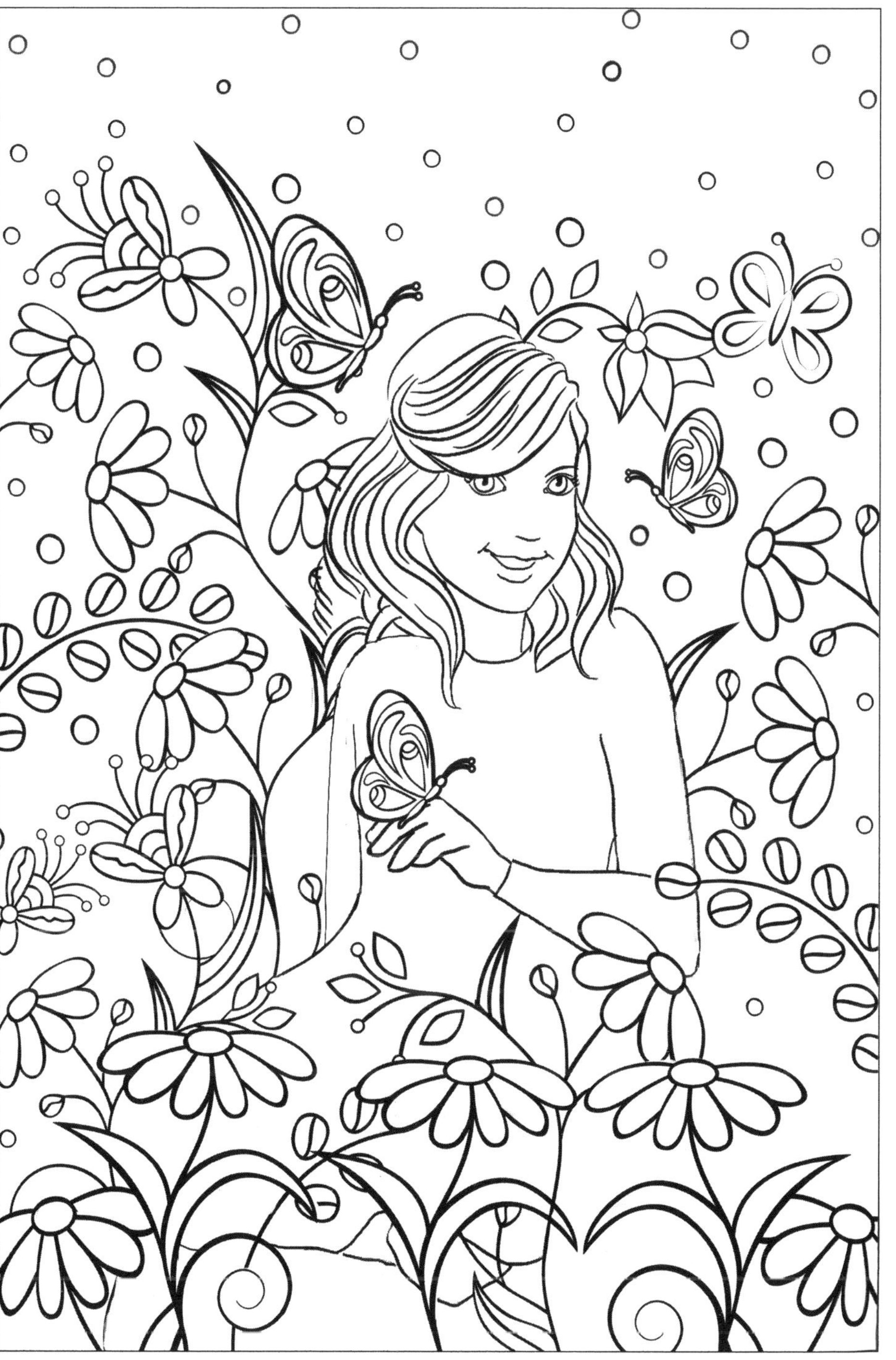

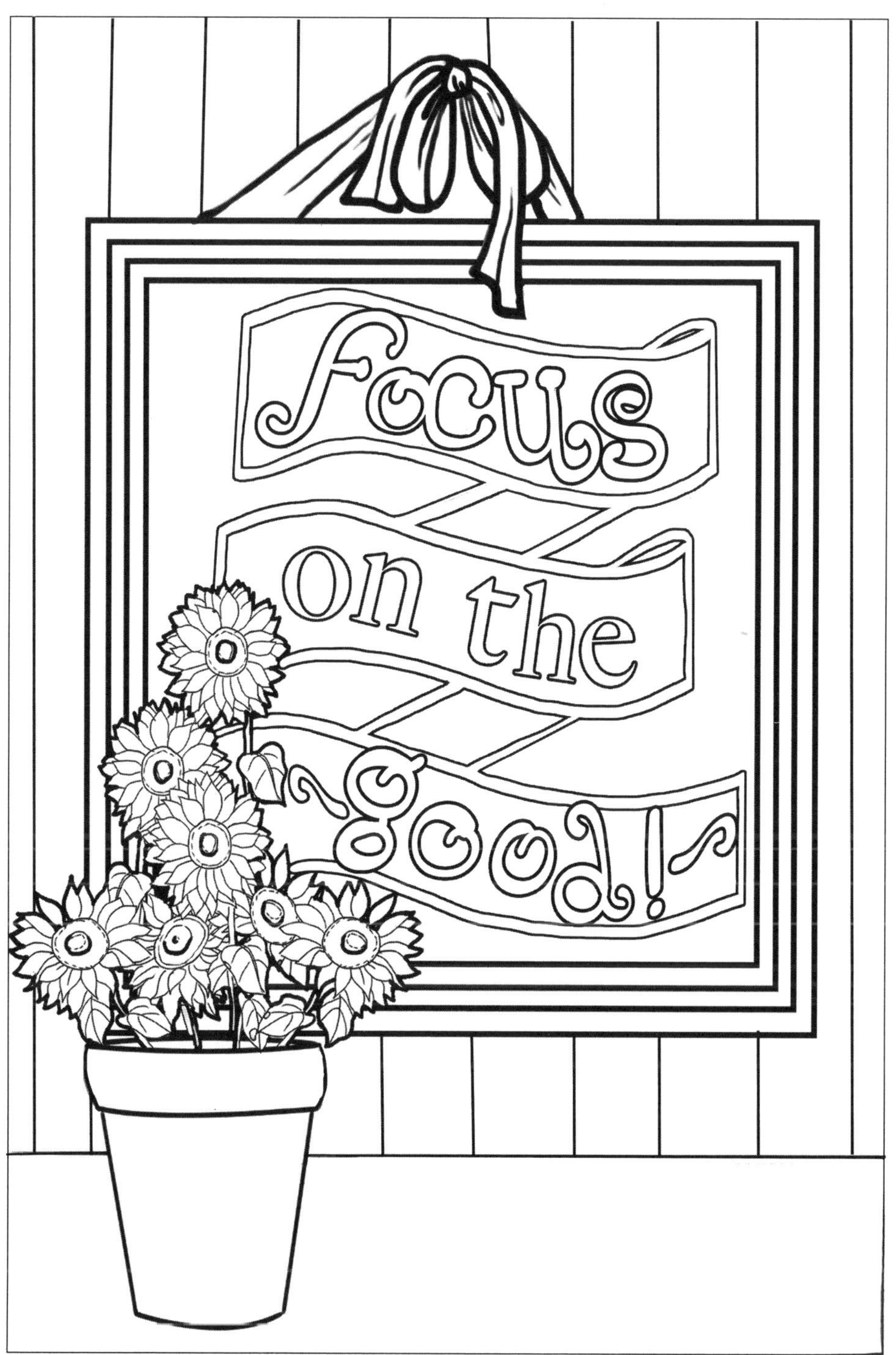
Focus
on the
good!

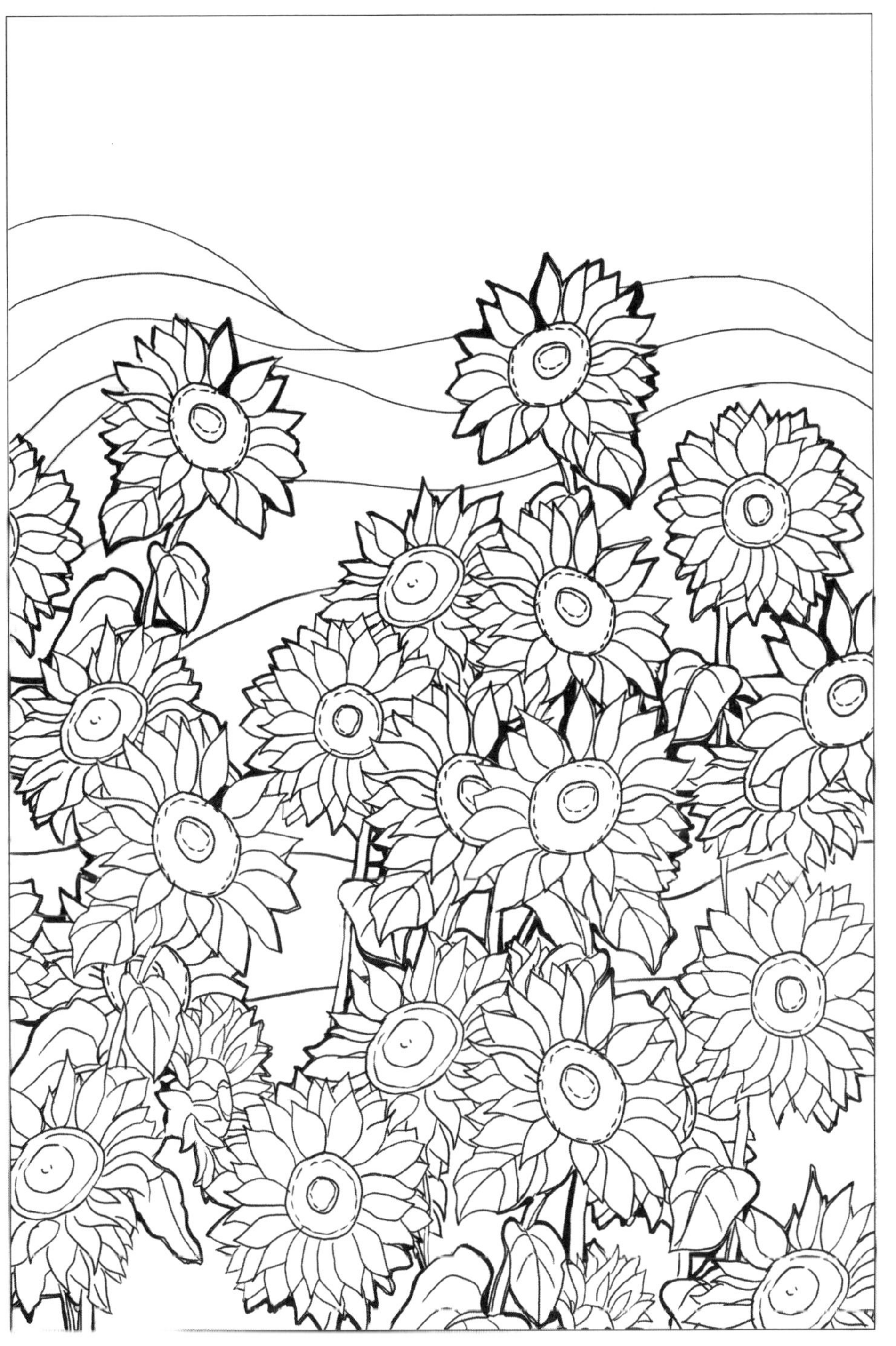

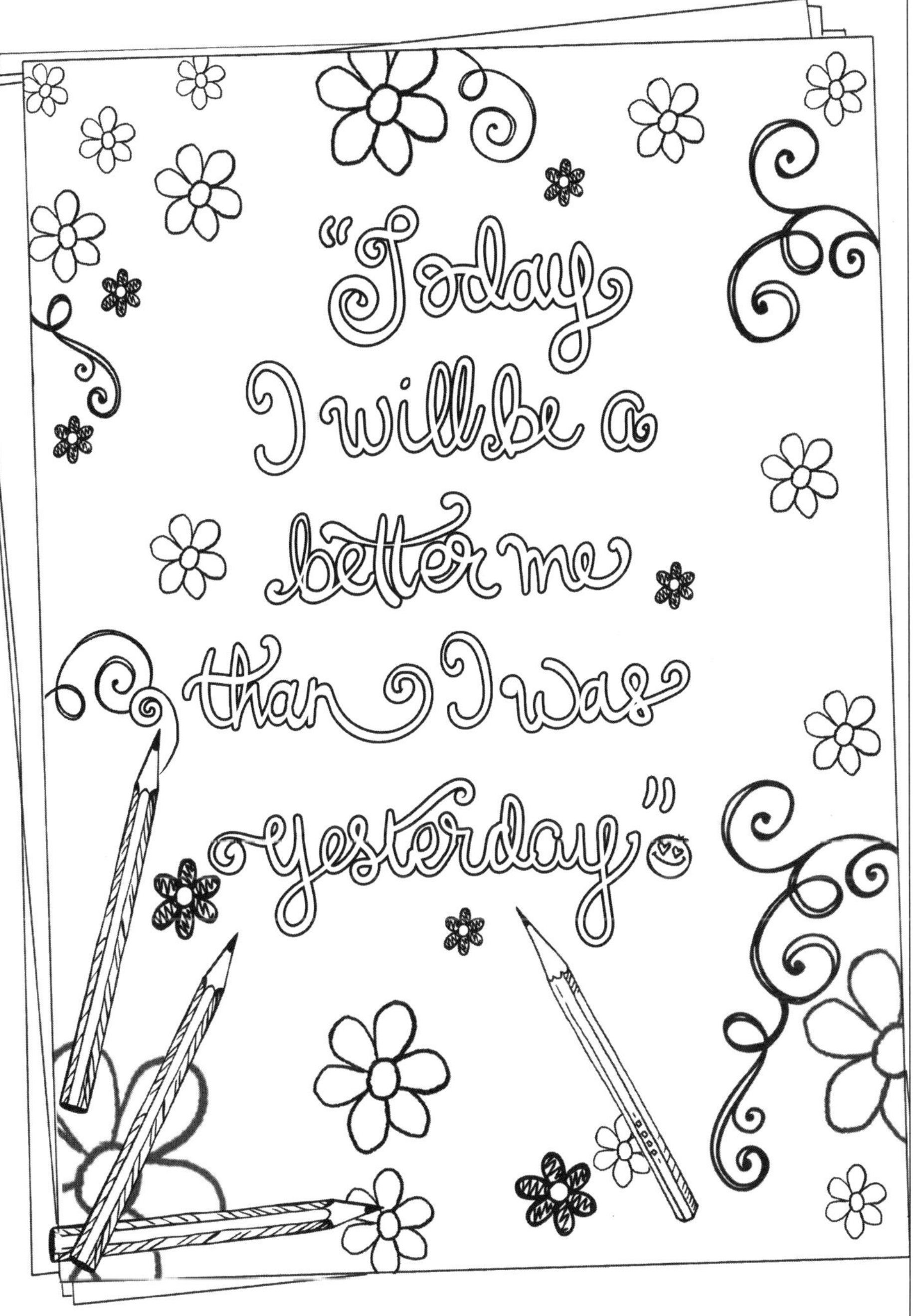
"Today
I will be a
better me
than I was
yesterday"

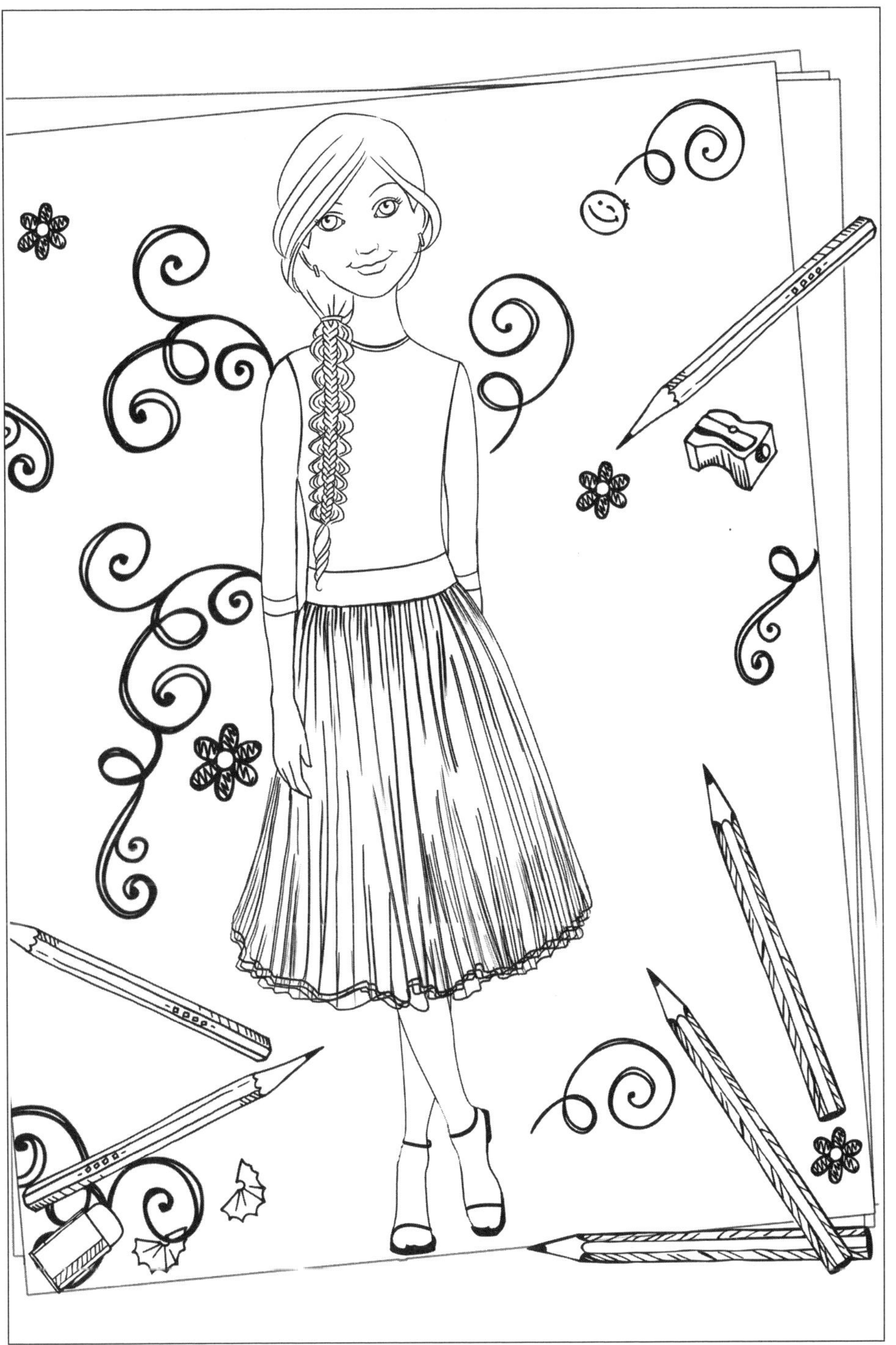

"How cool is it that G-d who created mountains and oceans and galaxies looked at you and thought the world needed one of you too!"

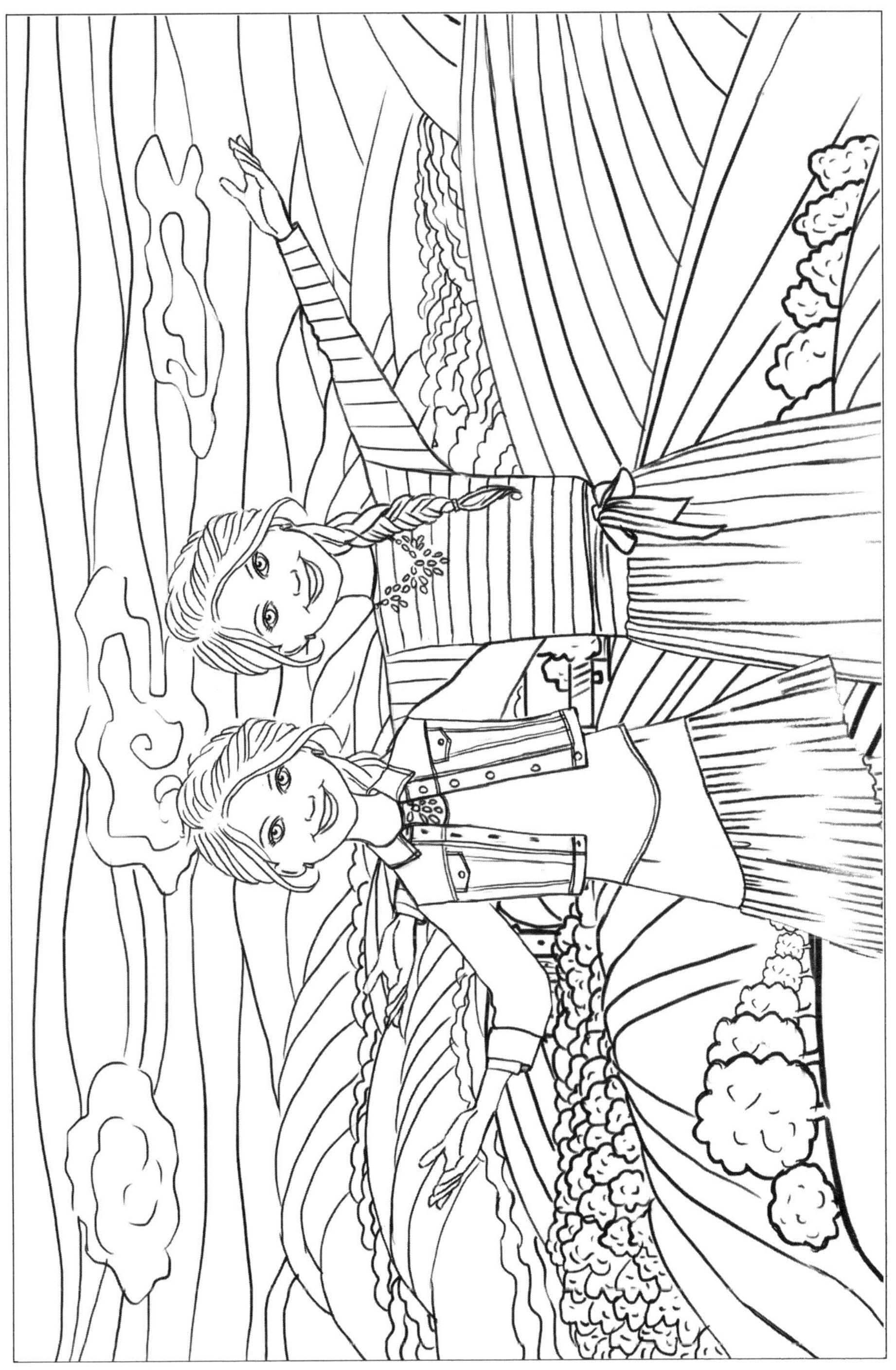

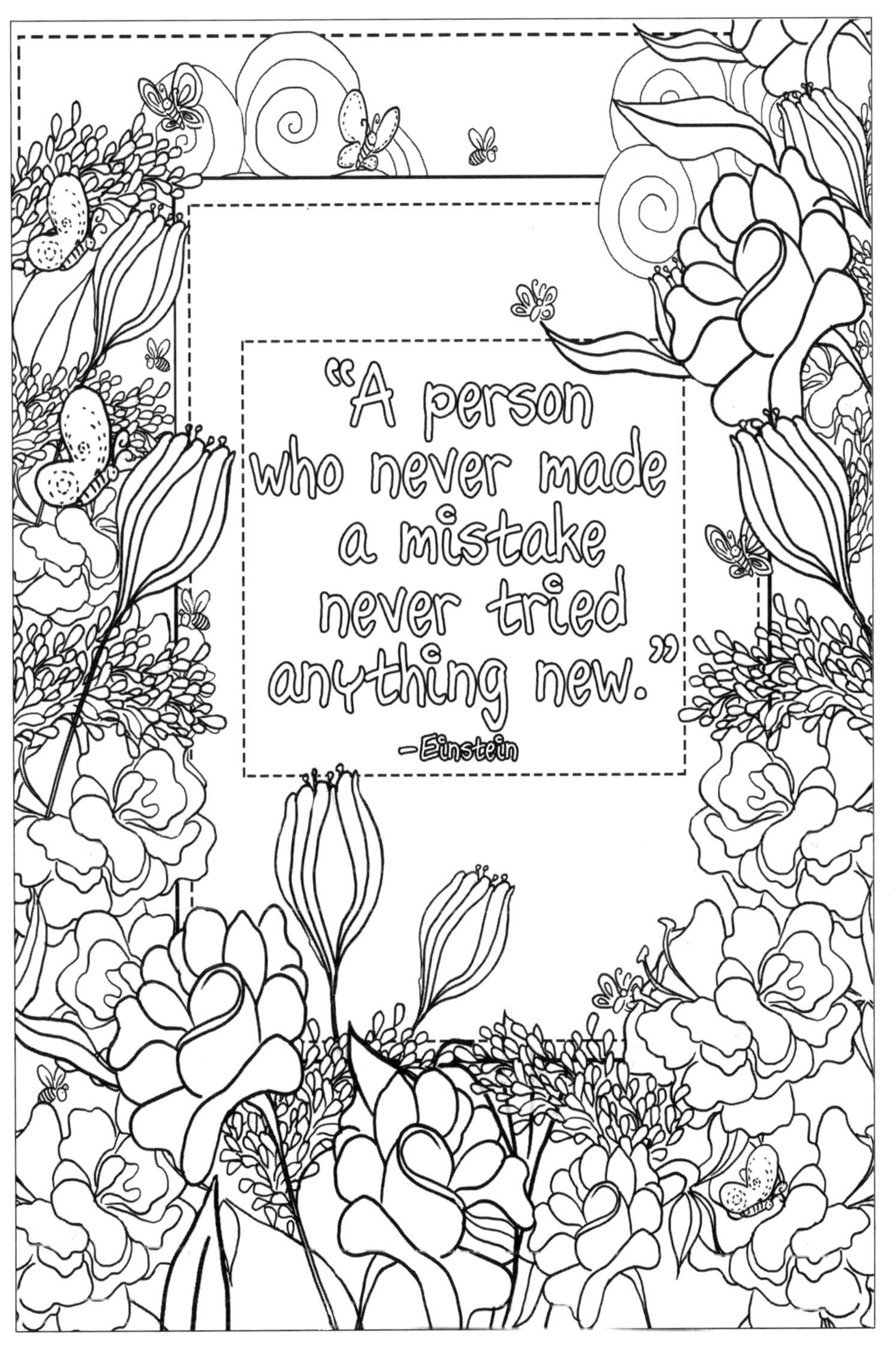
"A person
who never made
a mistake
never tried
anything new."
-Einstein

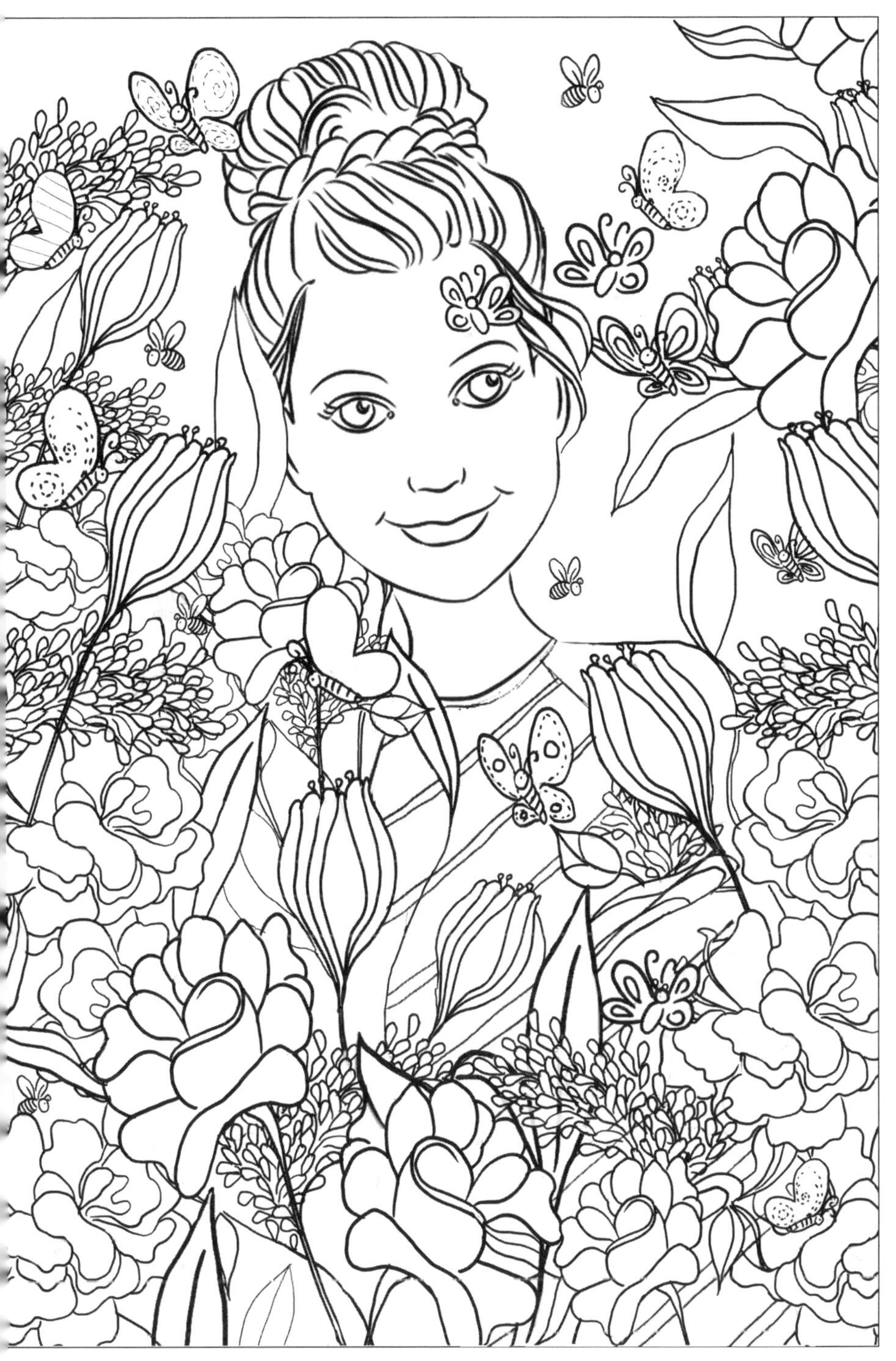

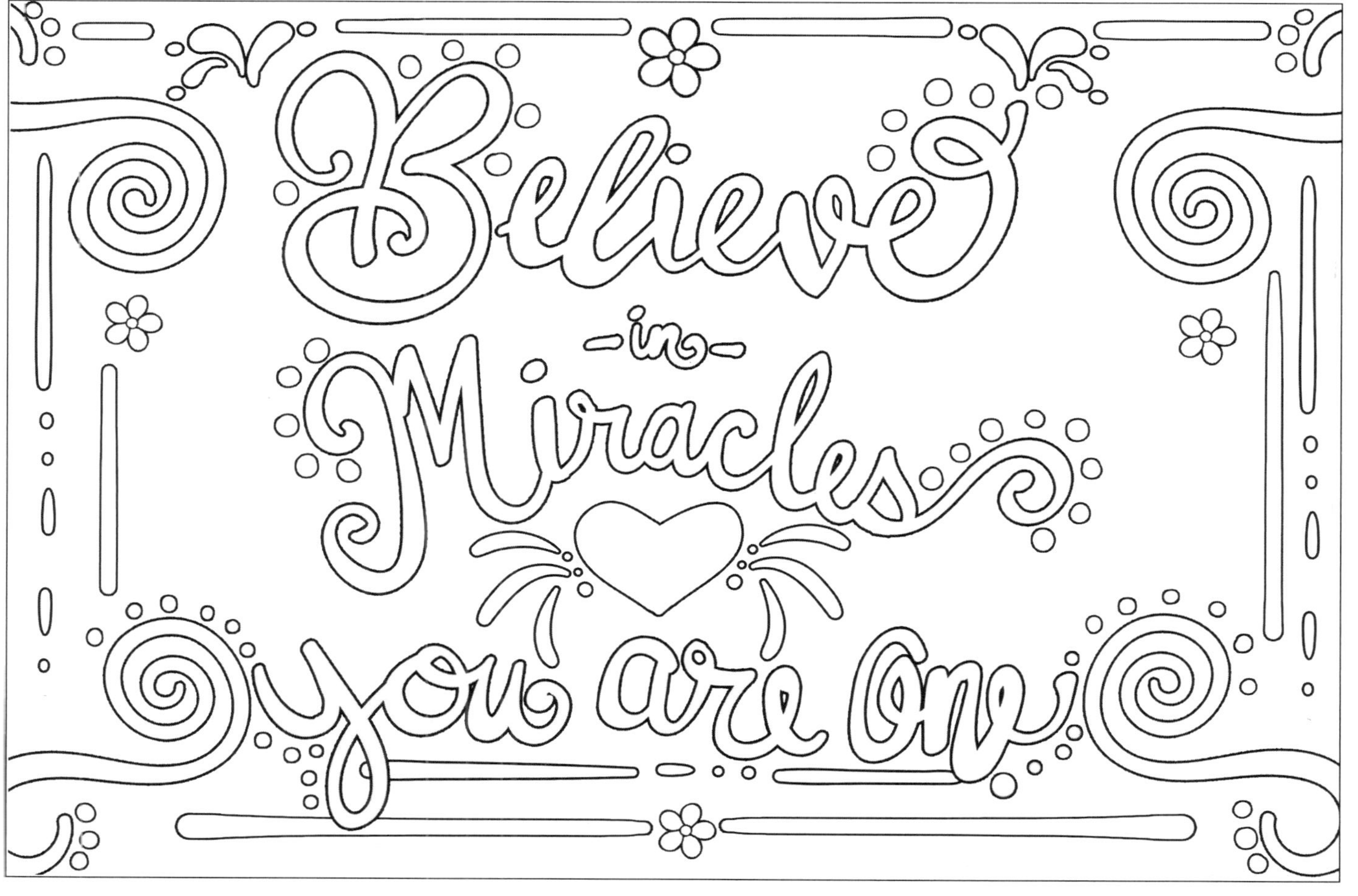
Believe
-in-
Miracles
you are one

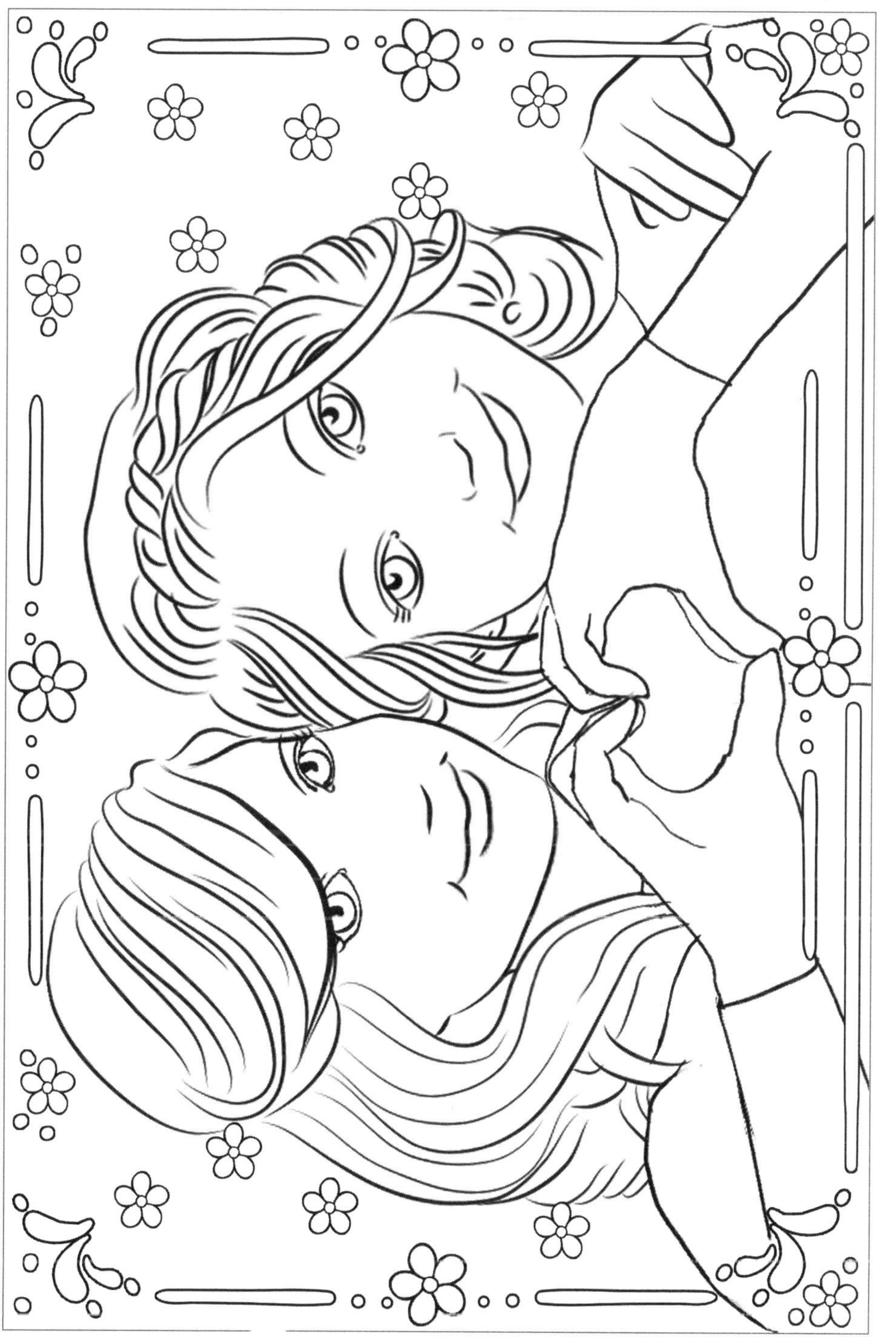

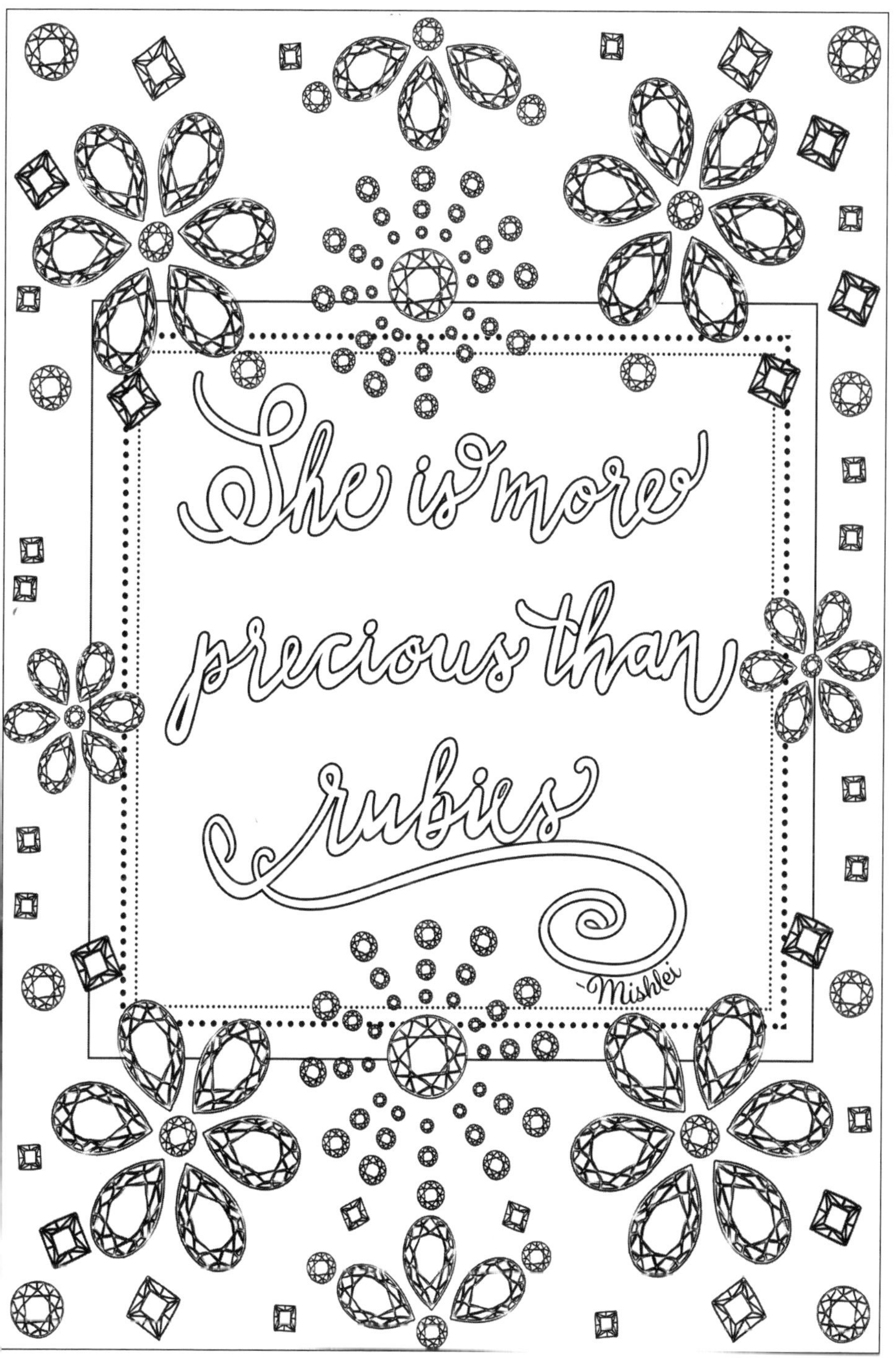
She is more precious than rubies
-Mishlei

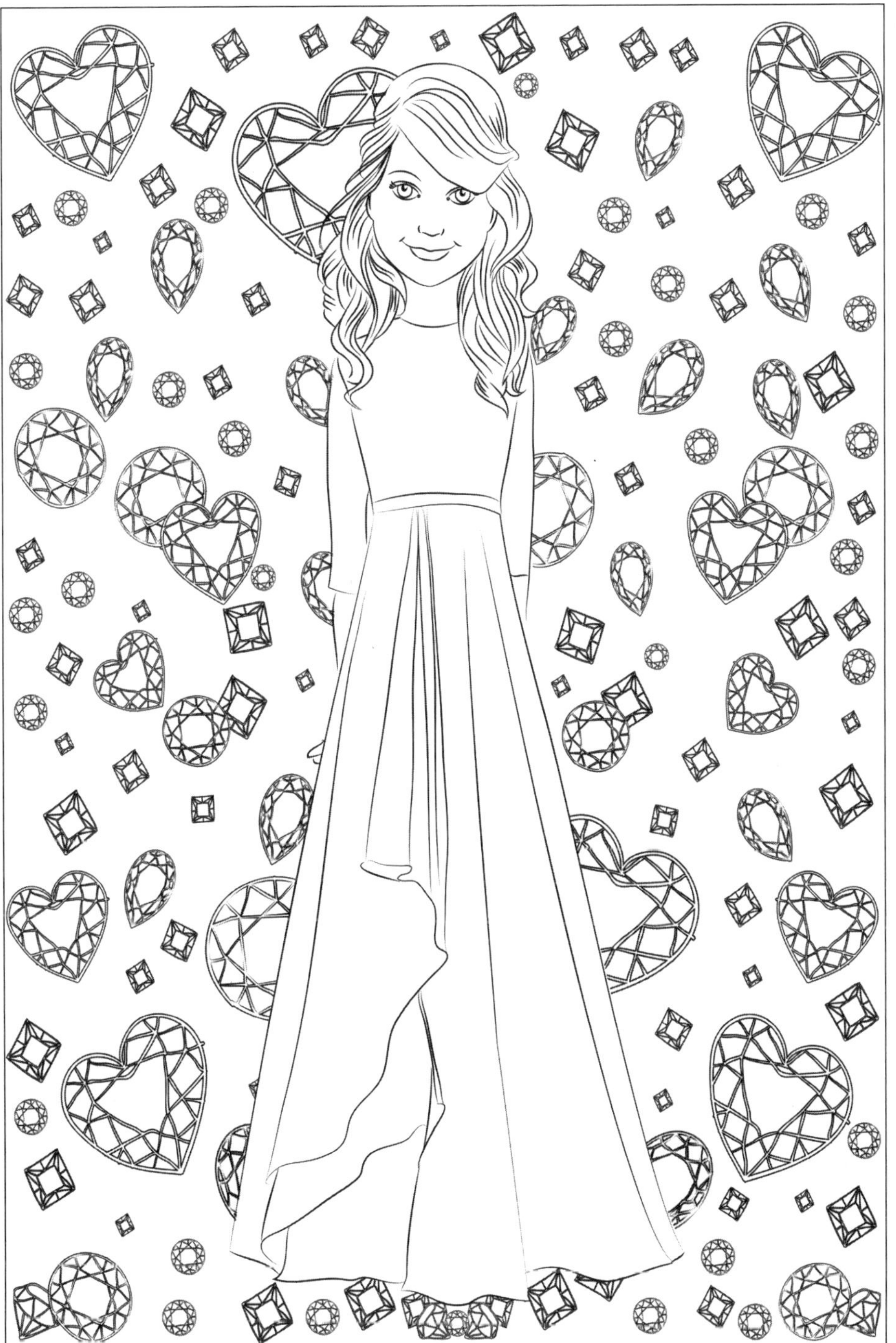

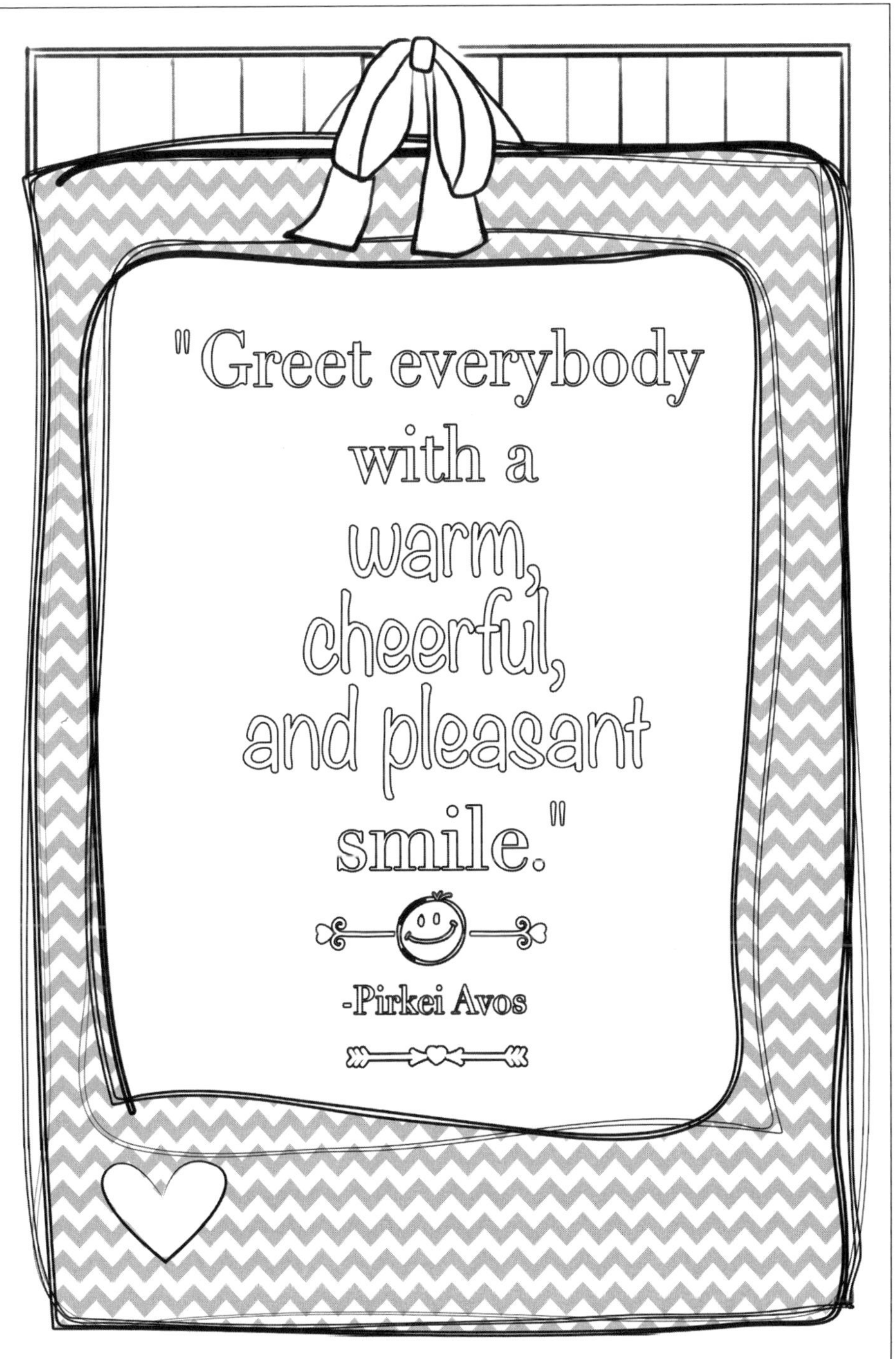
"Greet everybody
with a
warm,
cheerful,
and pleasant
smile."
-Pirkei Avos

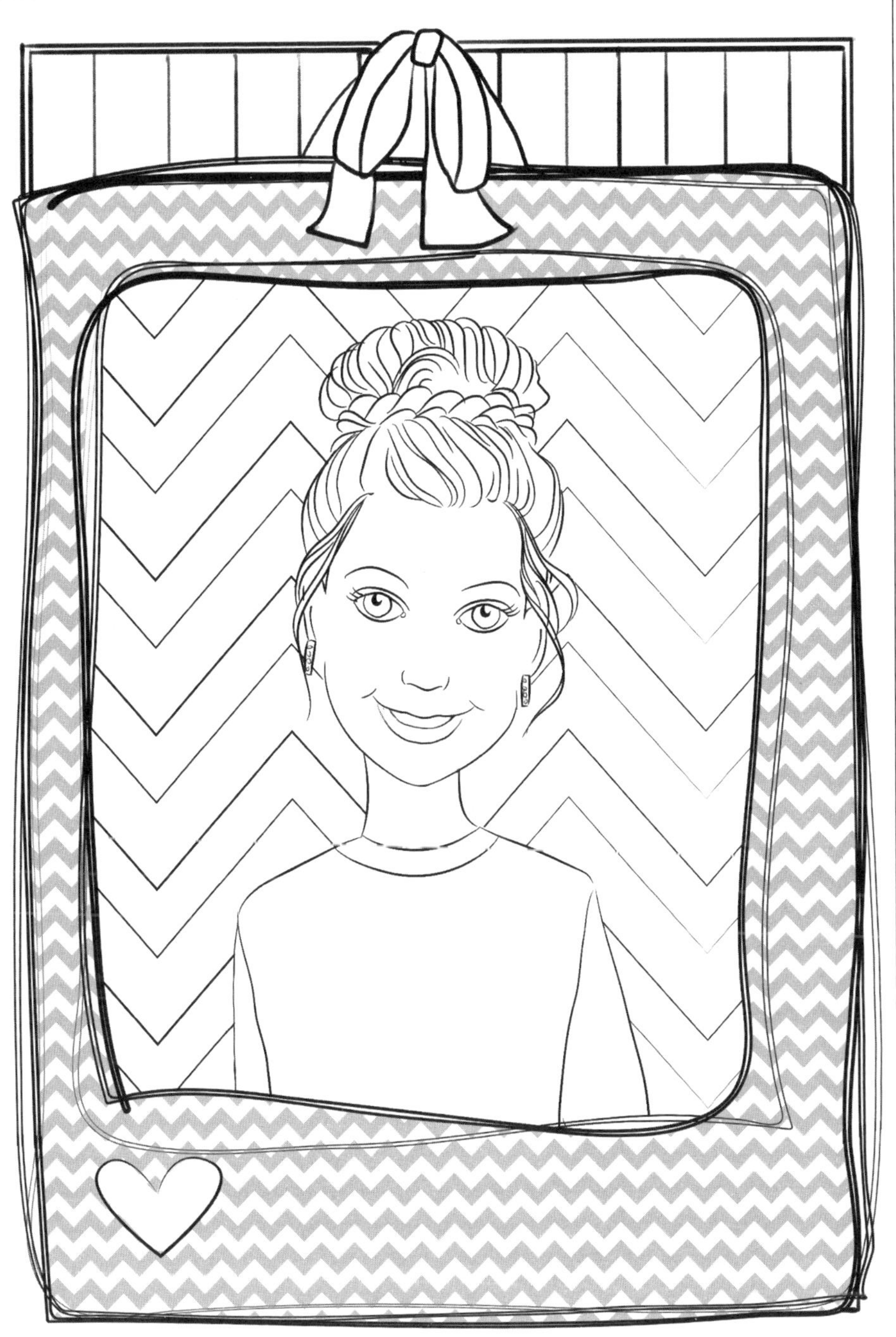

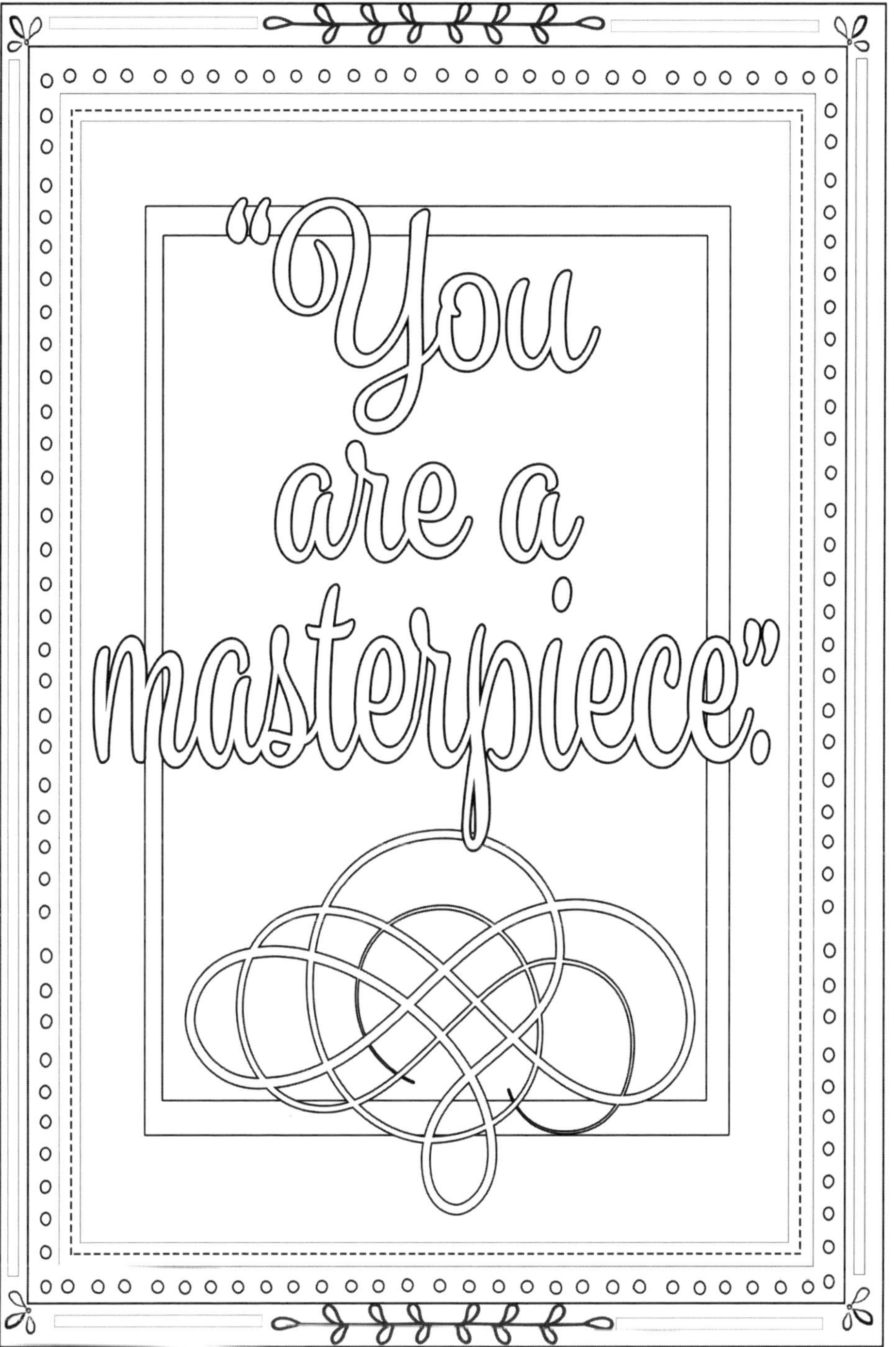
"You
are a
masterpiece".

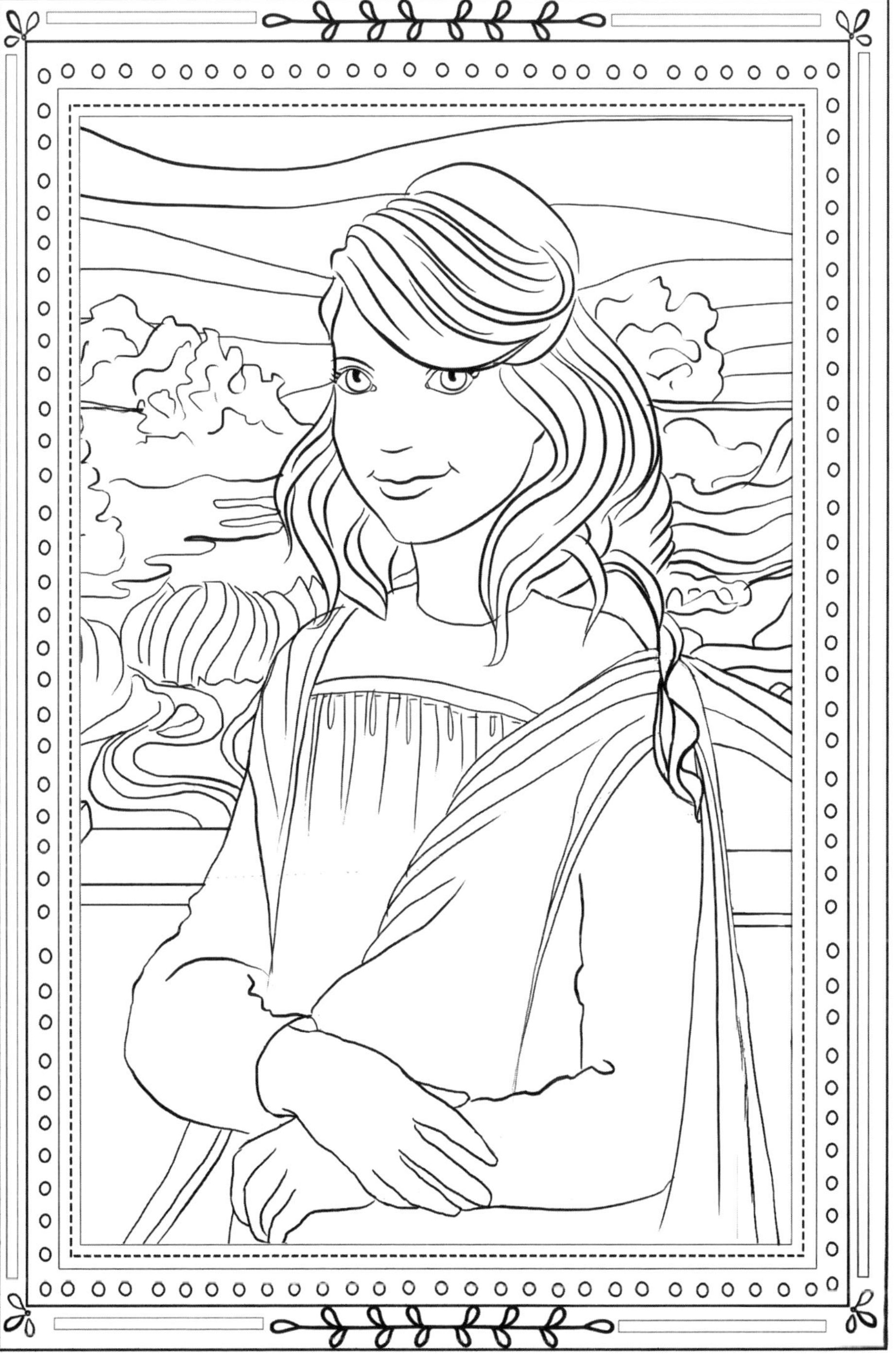

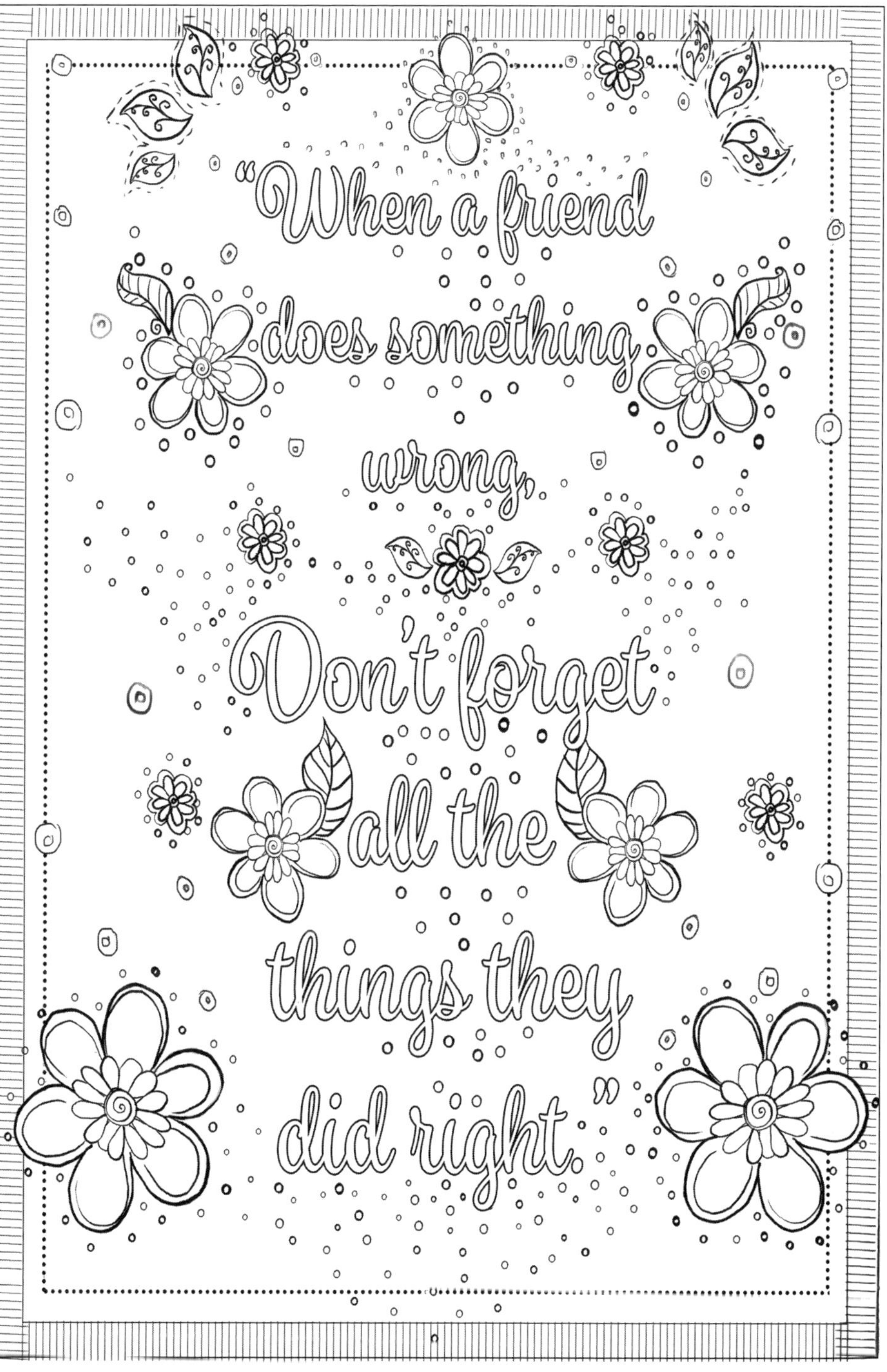
"When a friend
does something
wrong,
Don't forget
all the
things they
did right."

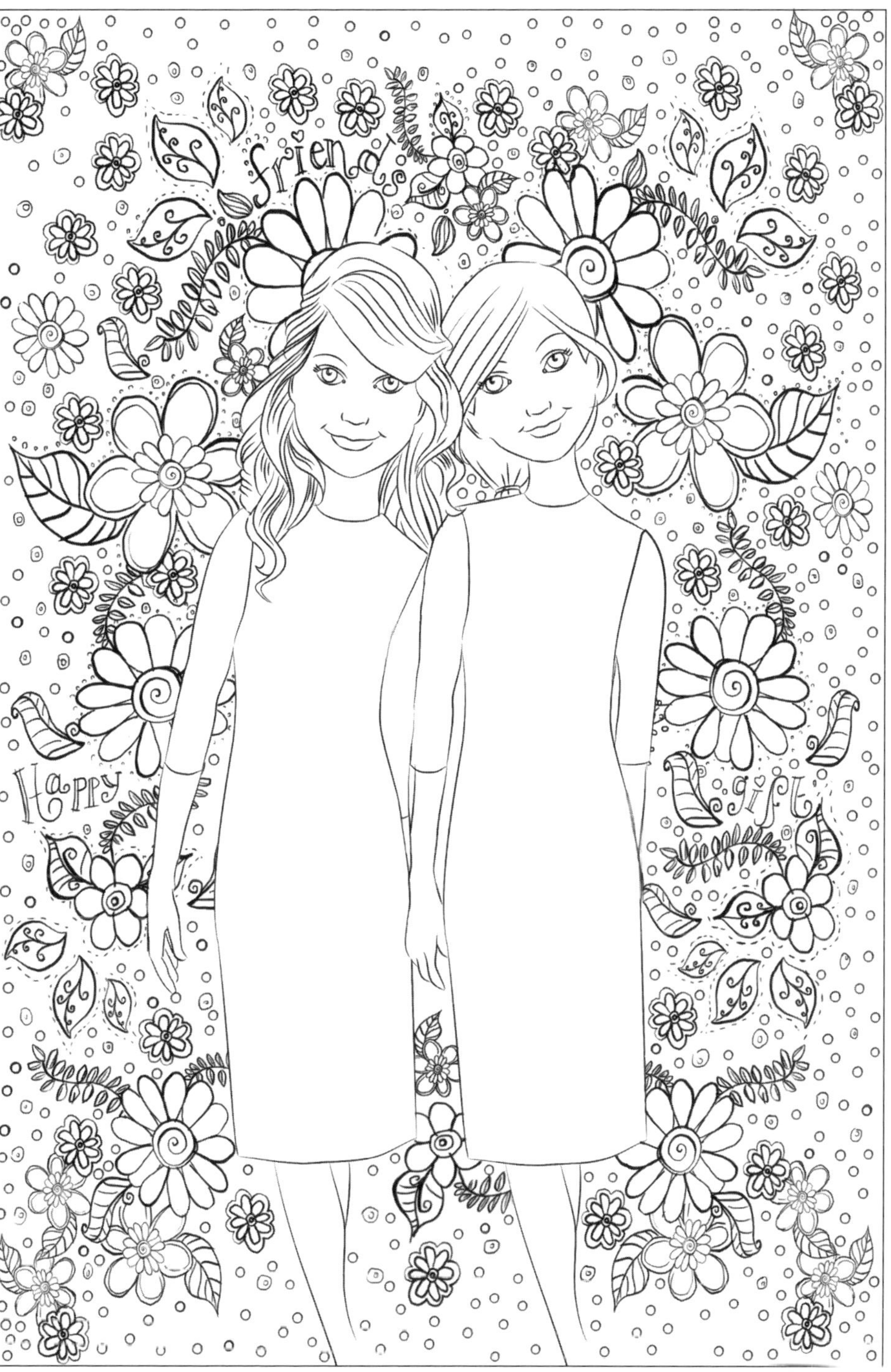
friends
Happy

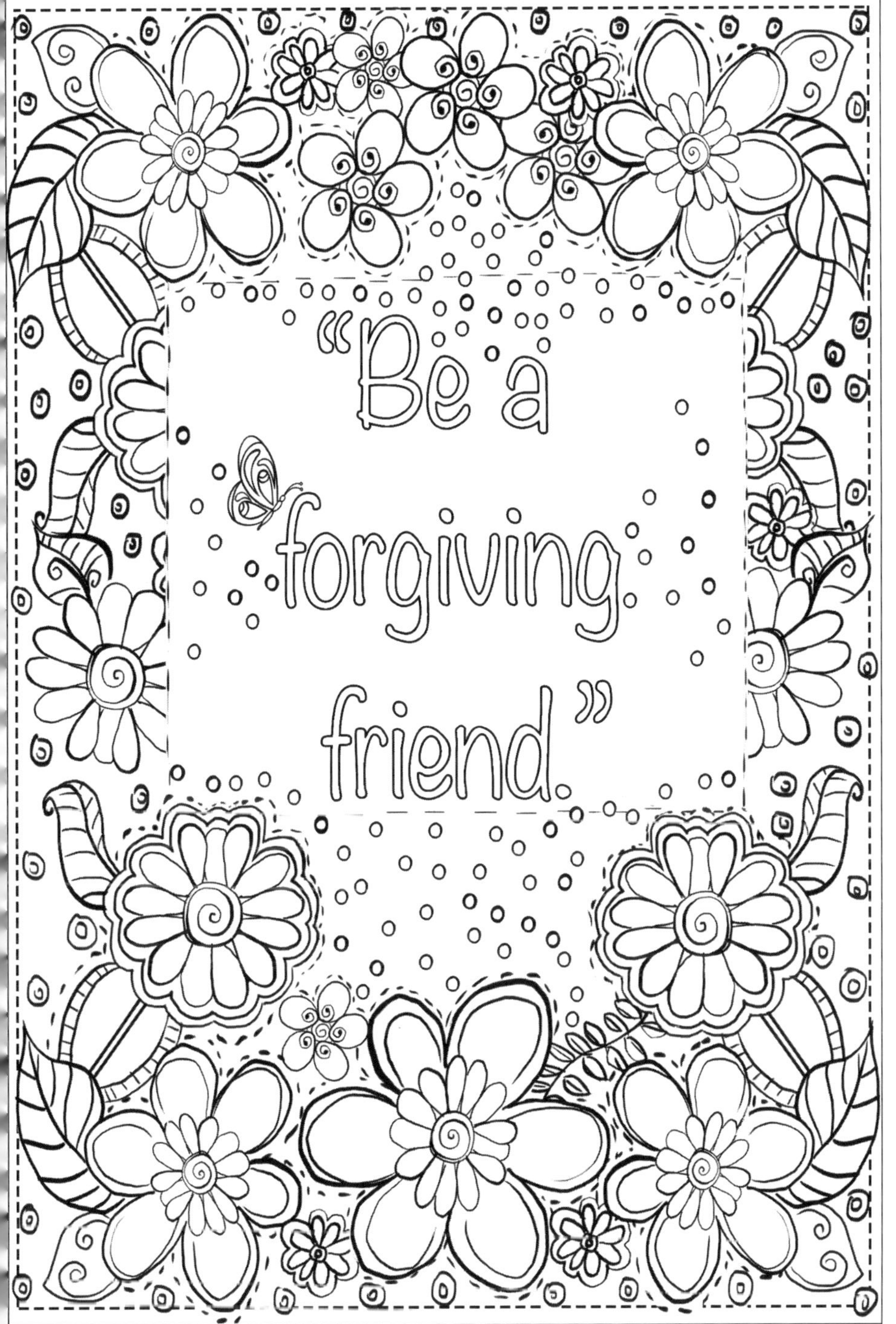
"Be a
forgiving
friend."

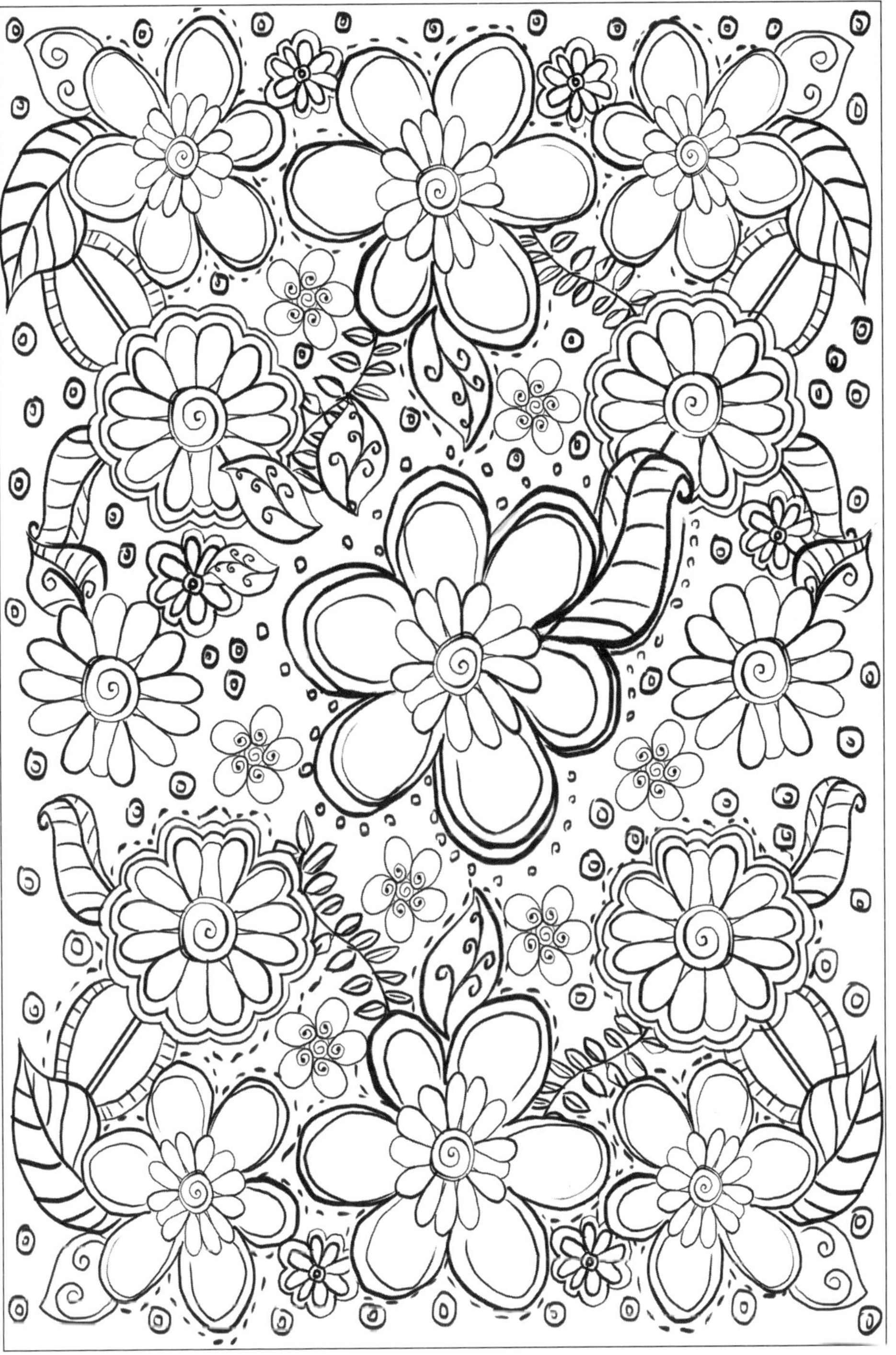

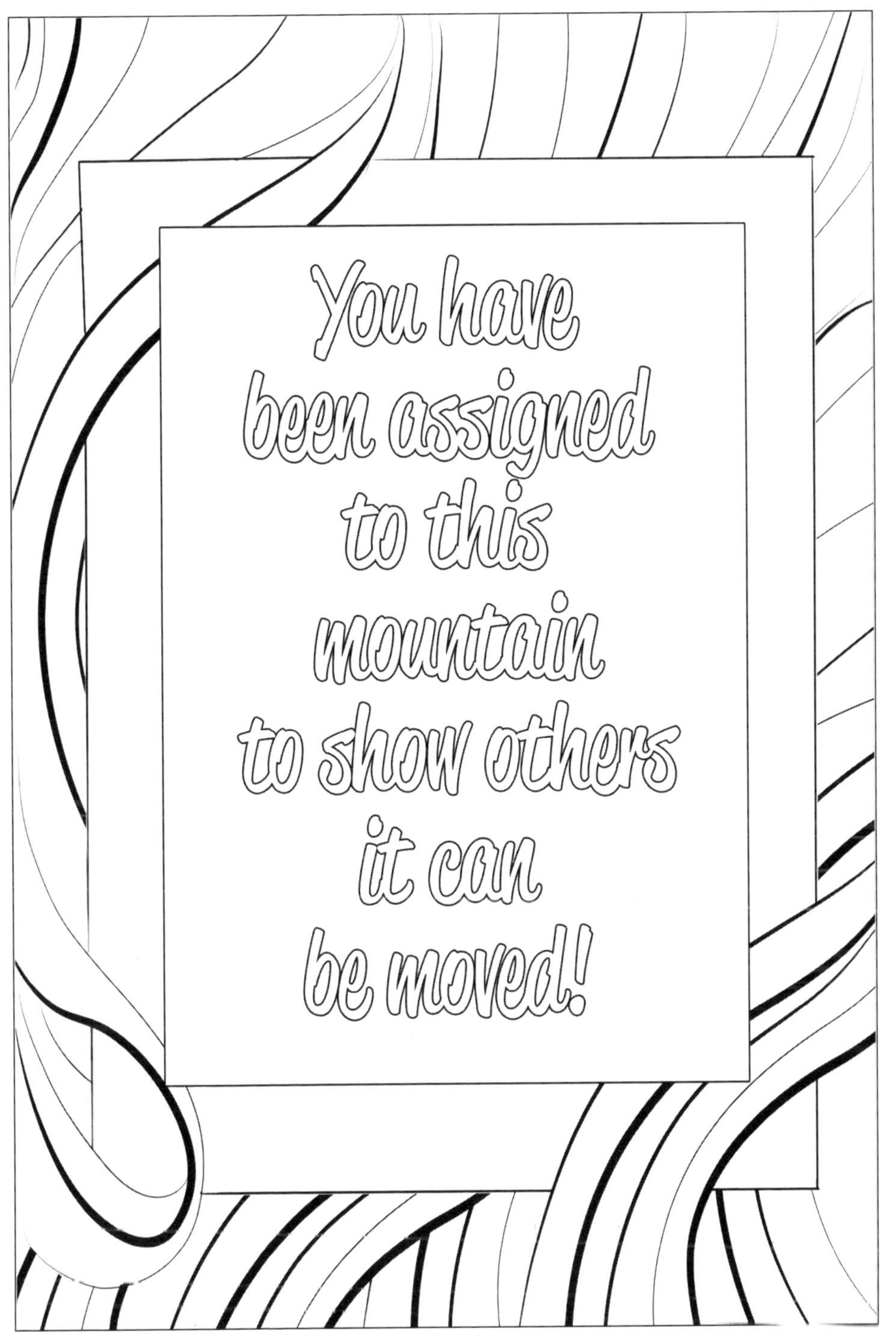
You have
been assigned
to this
mountain
to show others
it can
be moved!

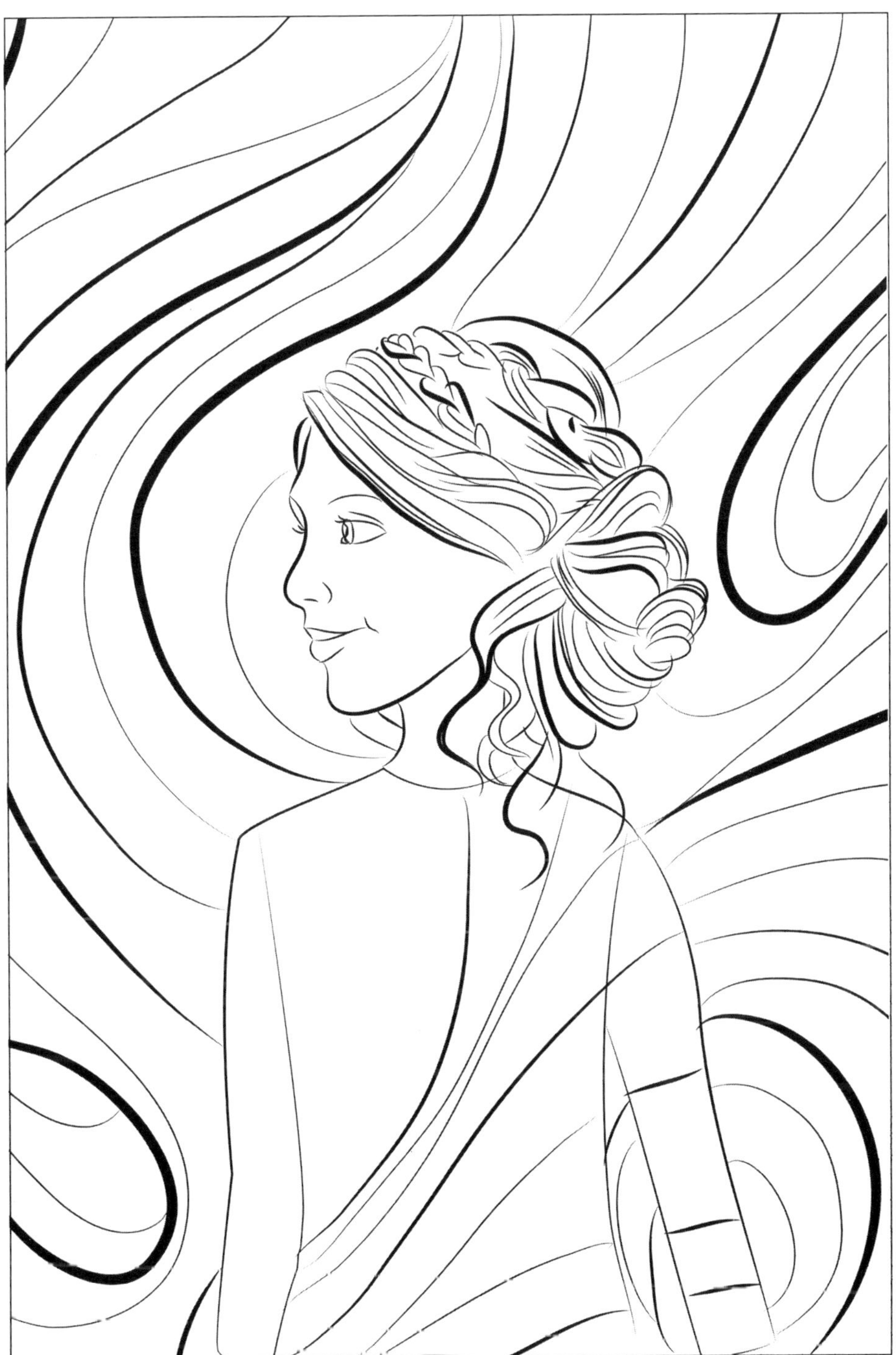

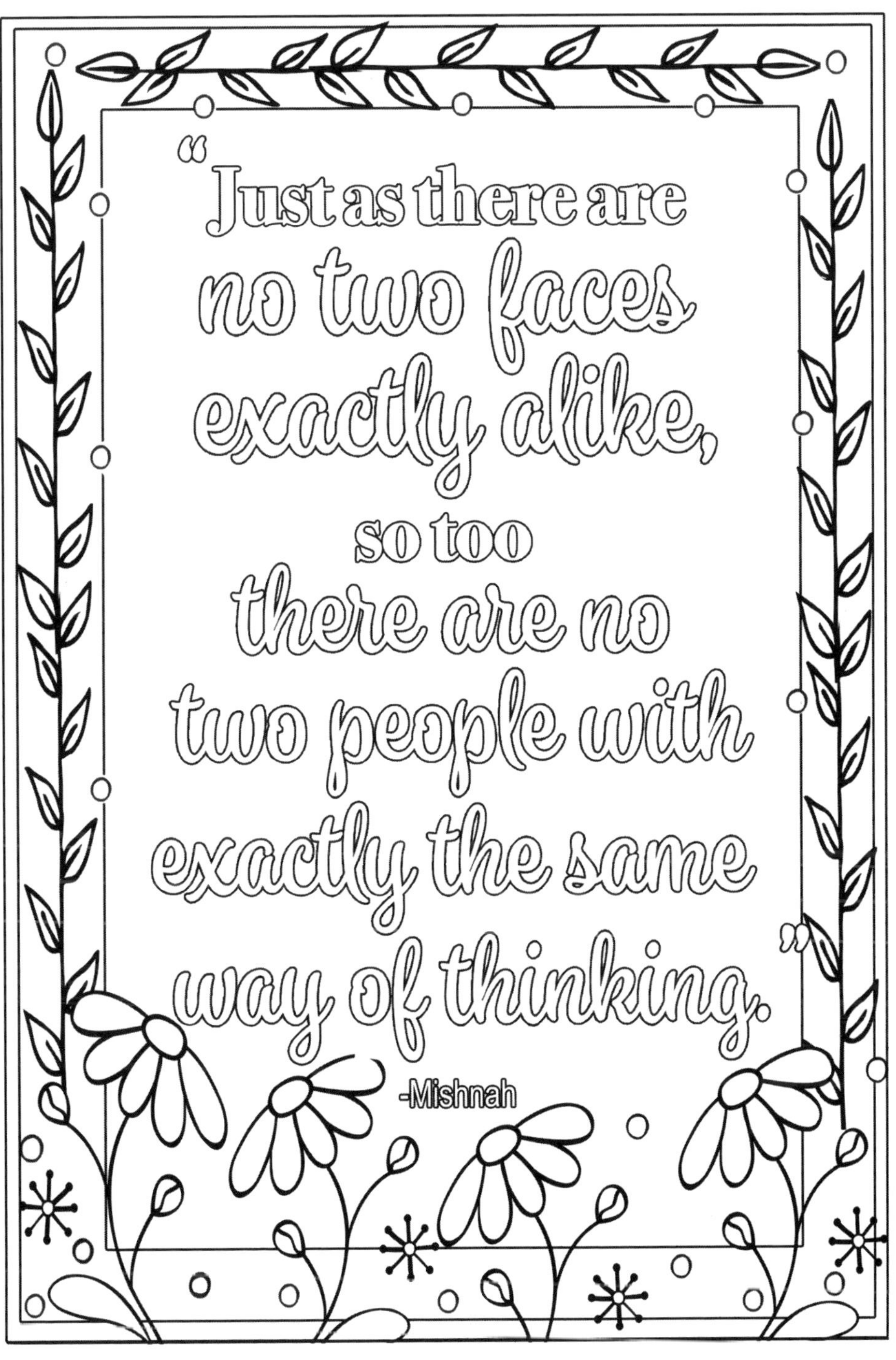
"Just as there are
no two faces
exactly alike,
so too
there are no
two people with
exactly the same
way of thinking."
-Mishnah

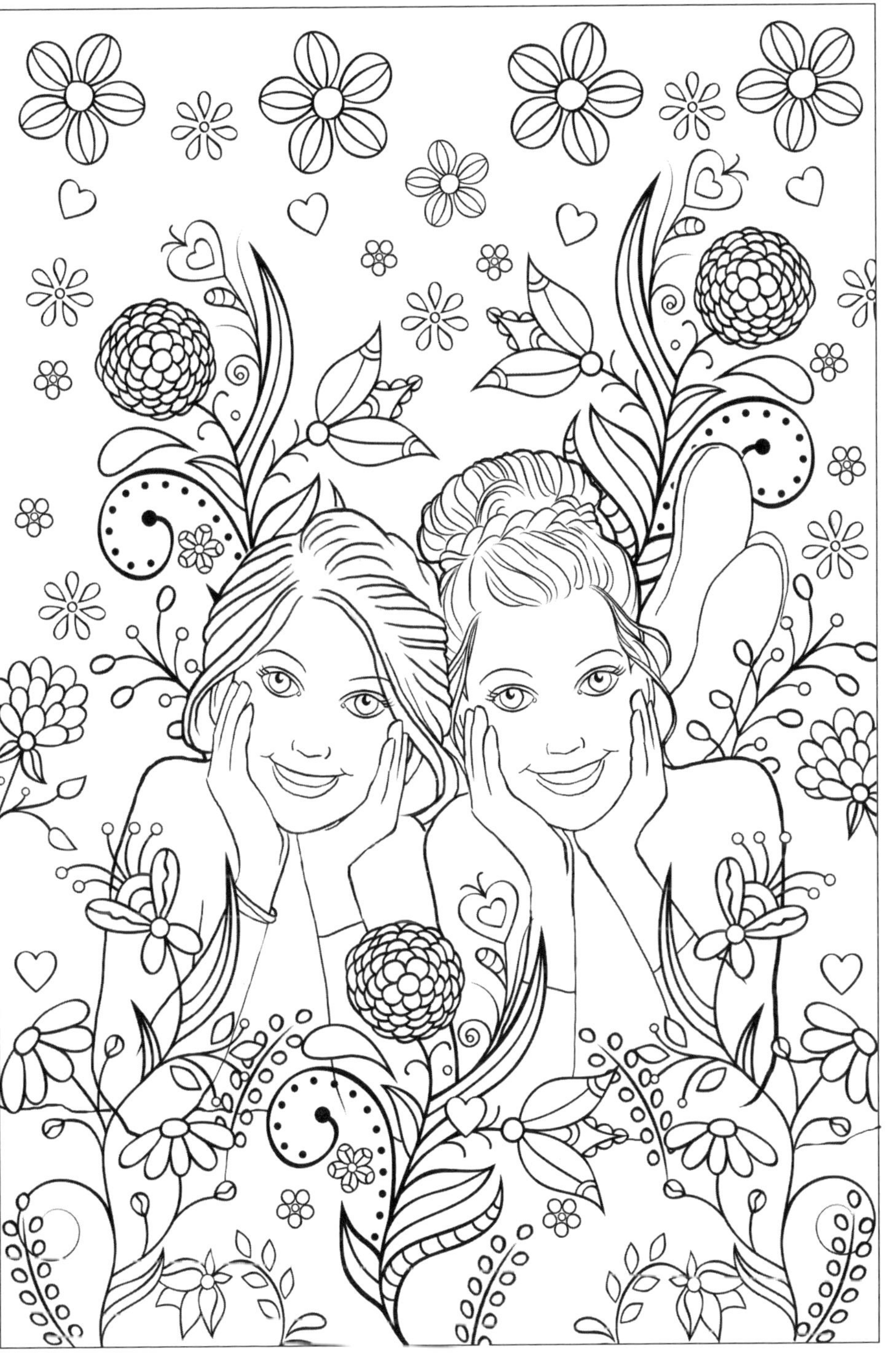

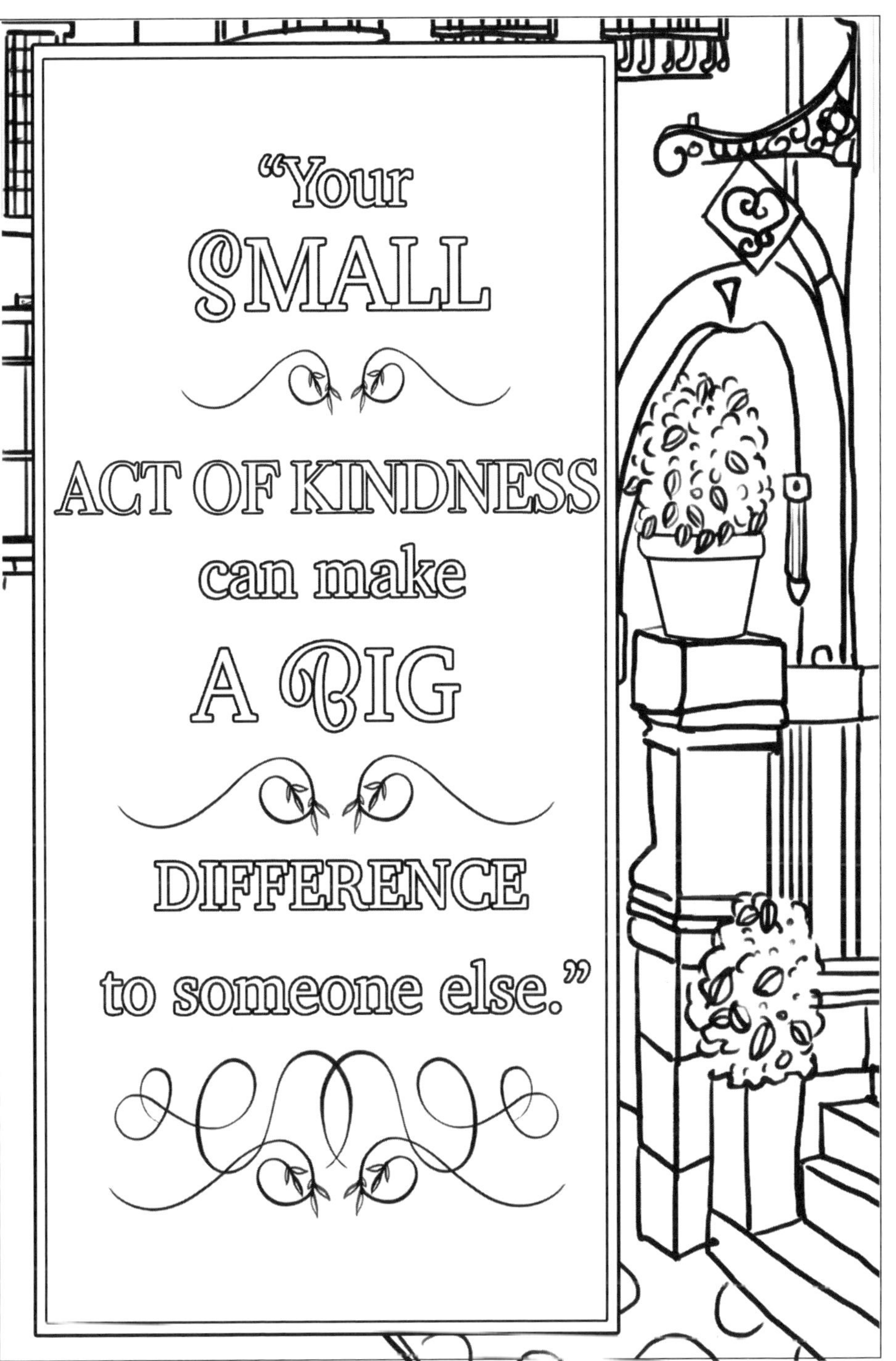
"Your
SMALL
ACT OF KINDNESS
can make
A BIG
DIFFERENCE
to someone else."

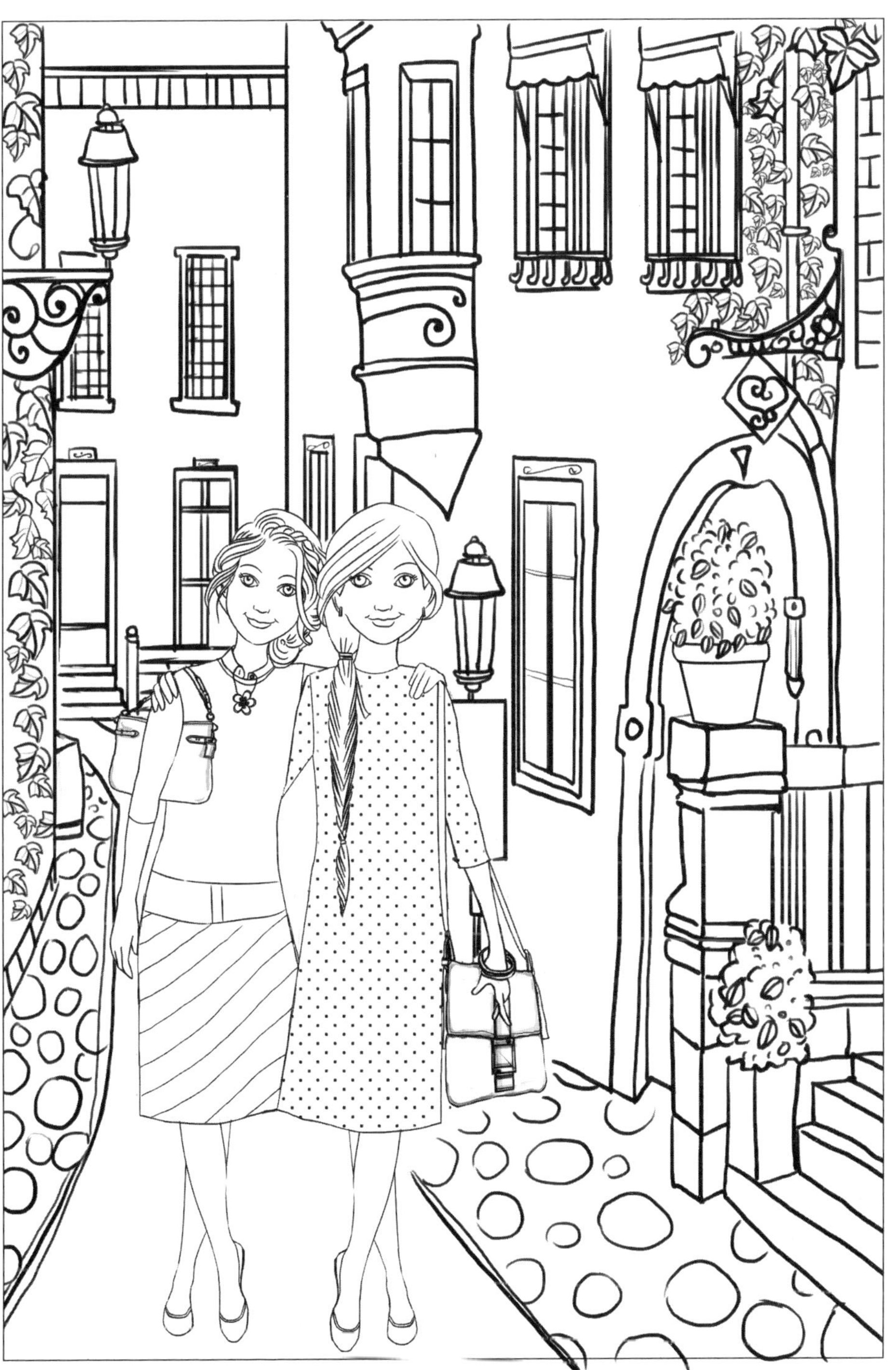

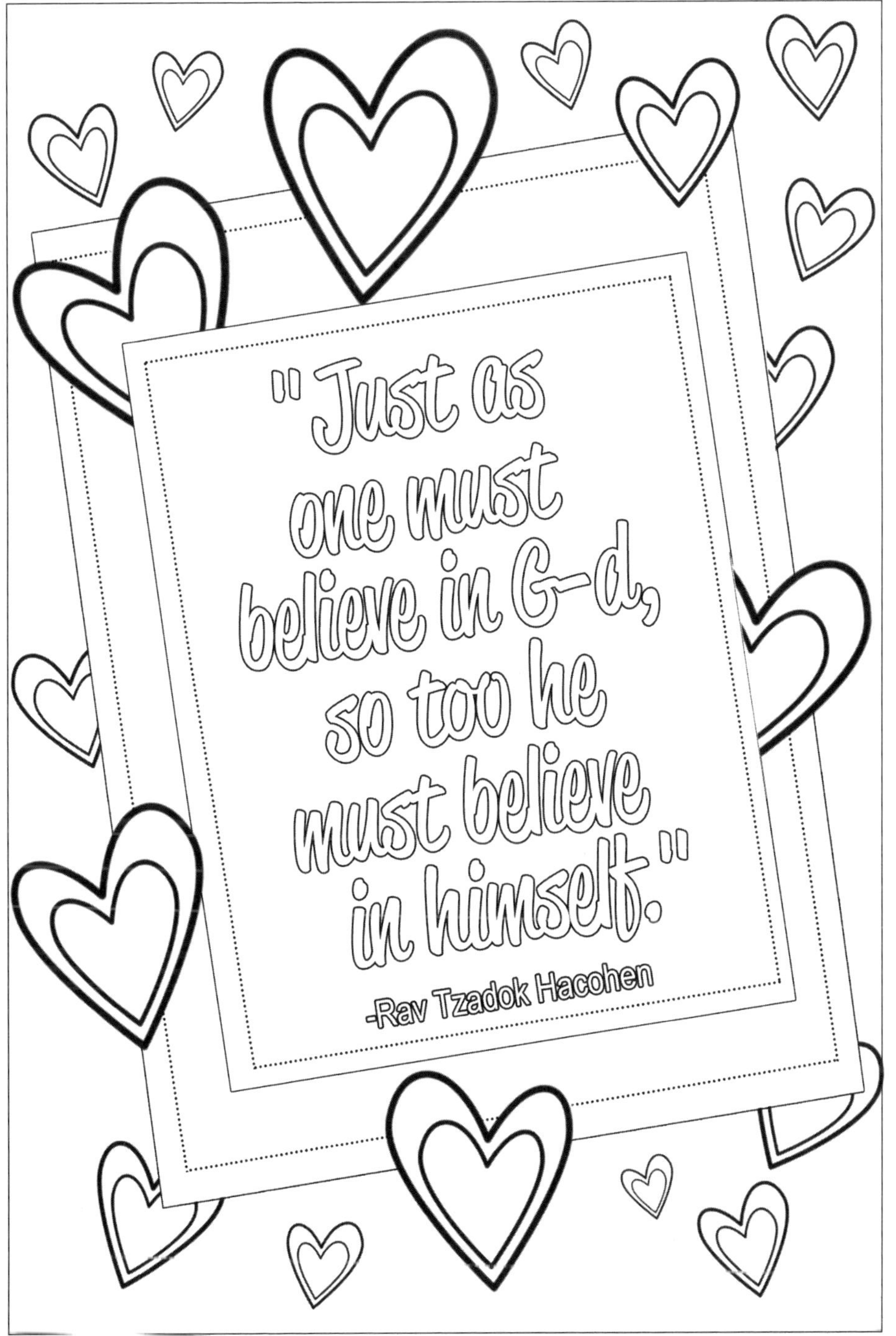
"Just as
one must
believe in G-d,
so too he
must believe
in himself."
-Rav Tzadok Hacohen

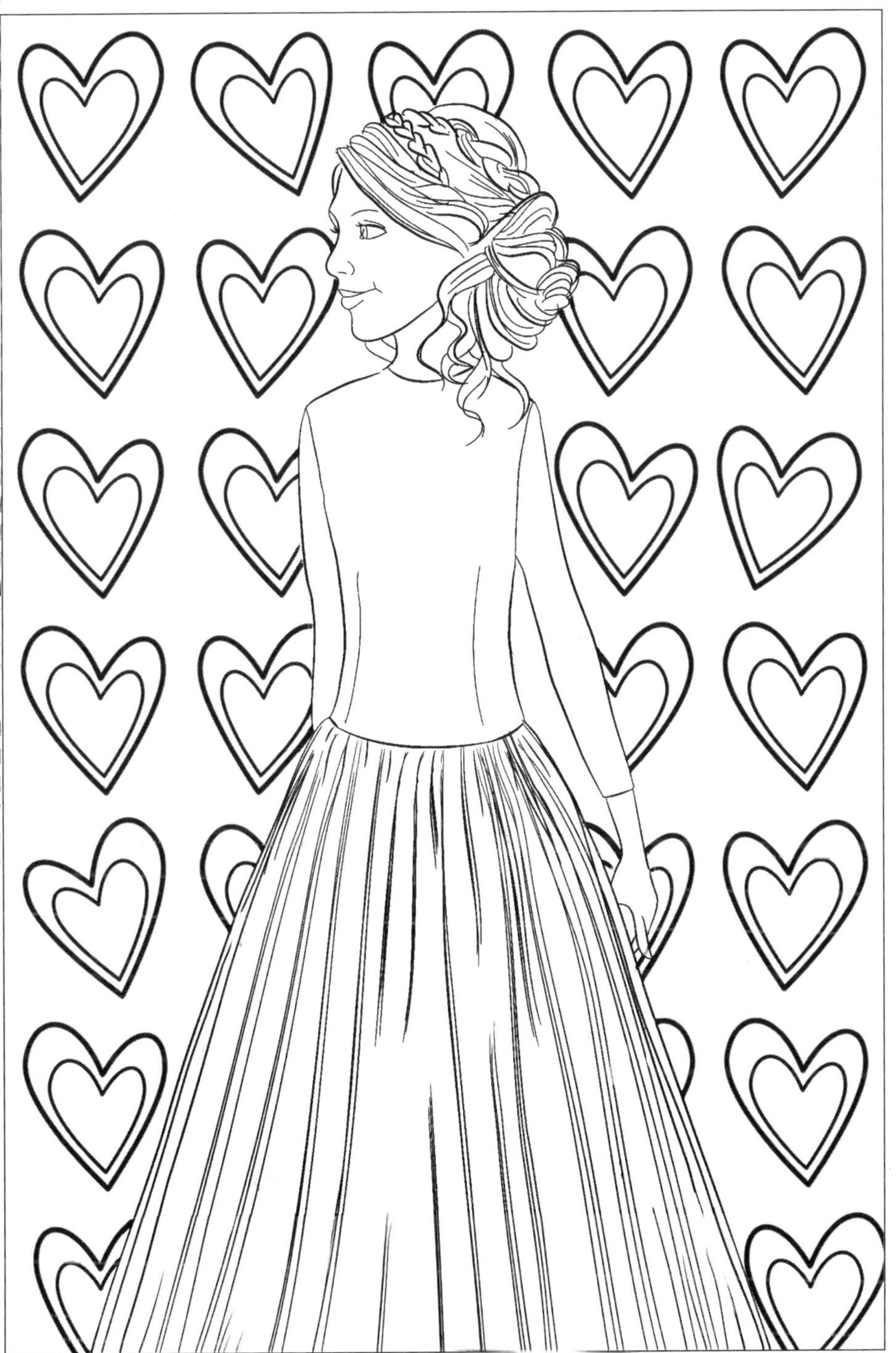

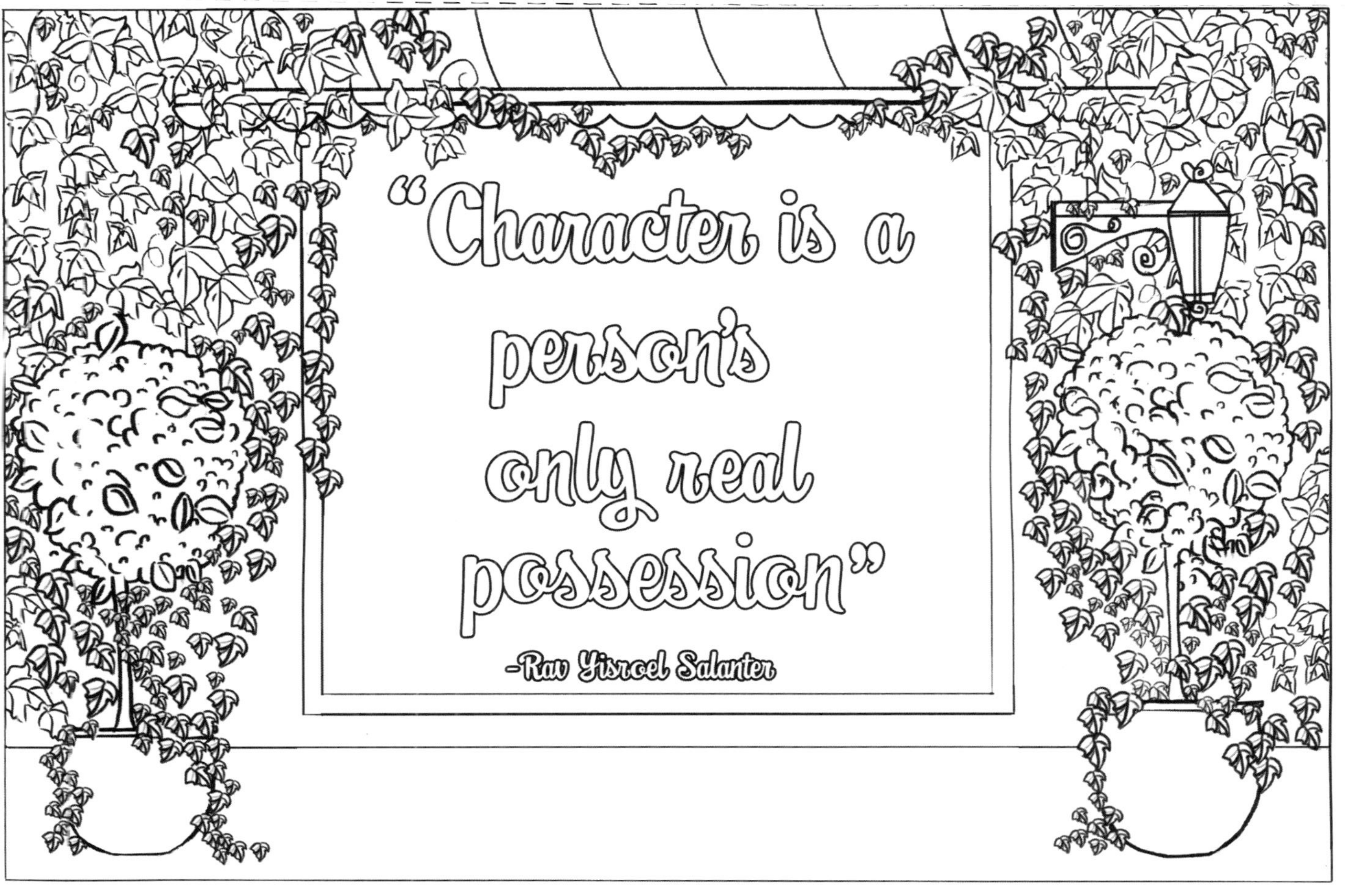
"Character is a
person's
only real
possession"
-Rav Yisroel Salanter

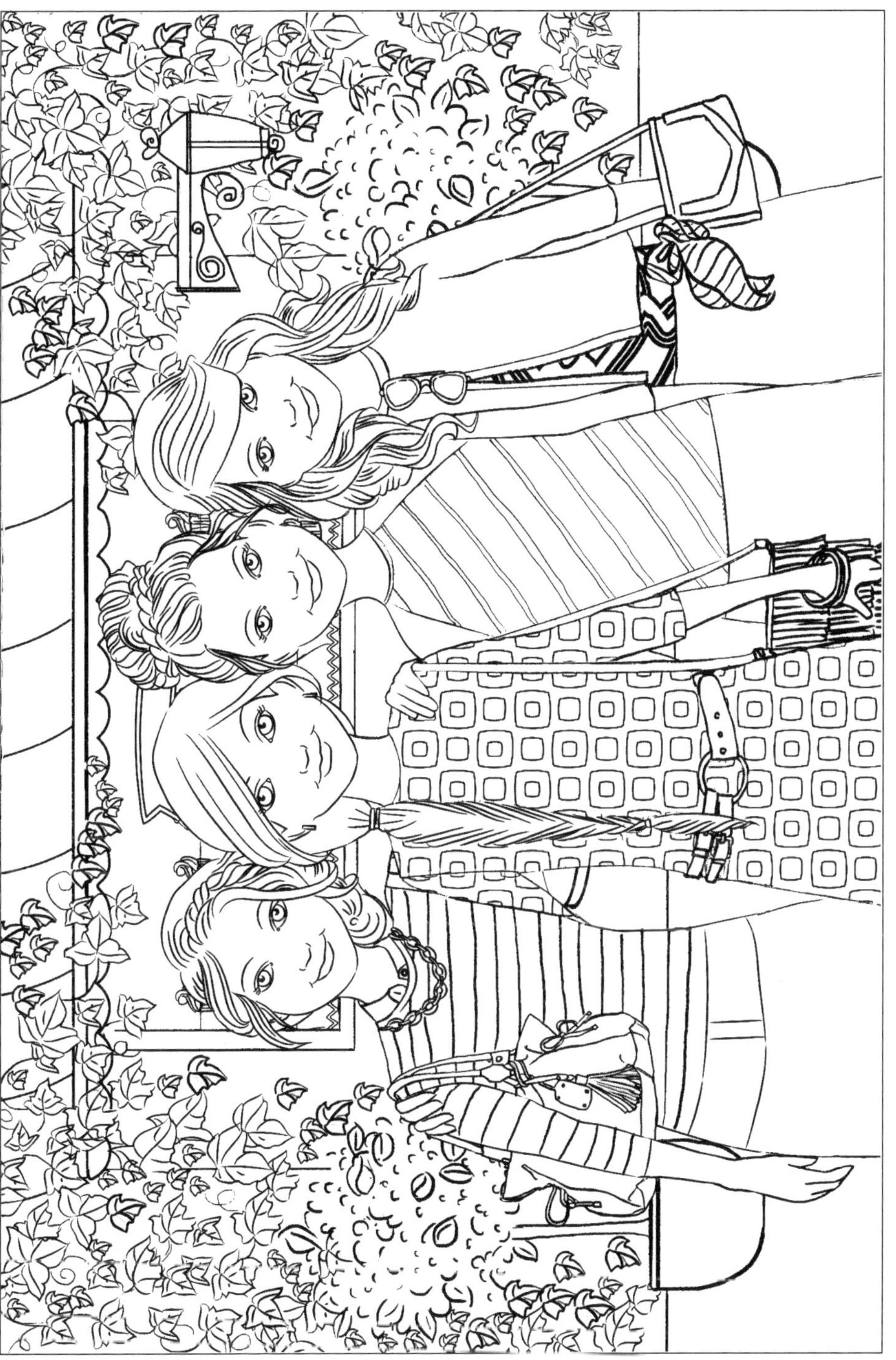

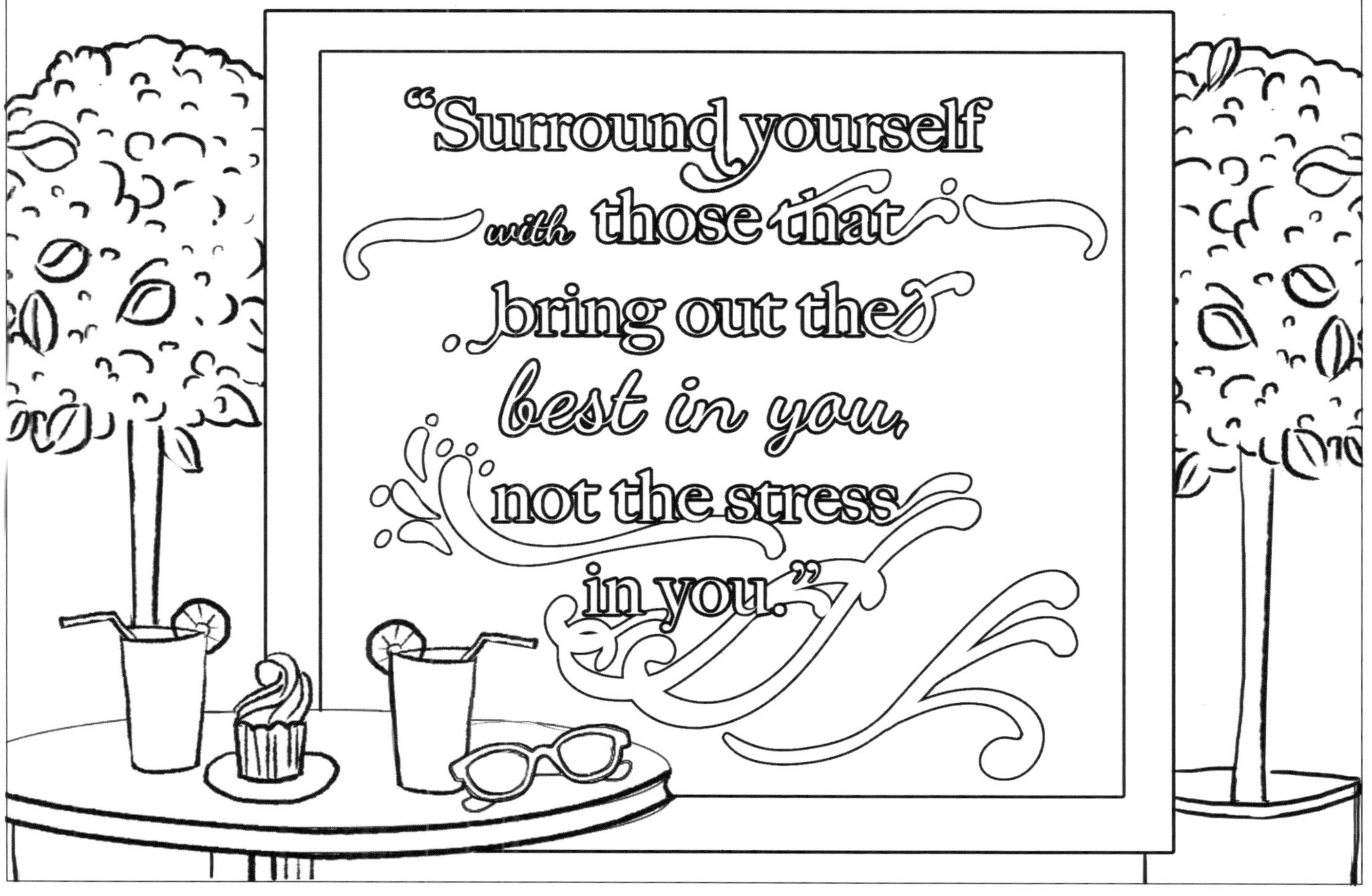
"Surround yourself
with those that
bring out the
best in you,
not the stress
in you."

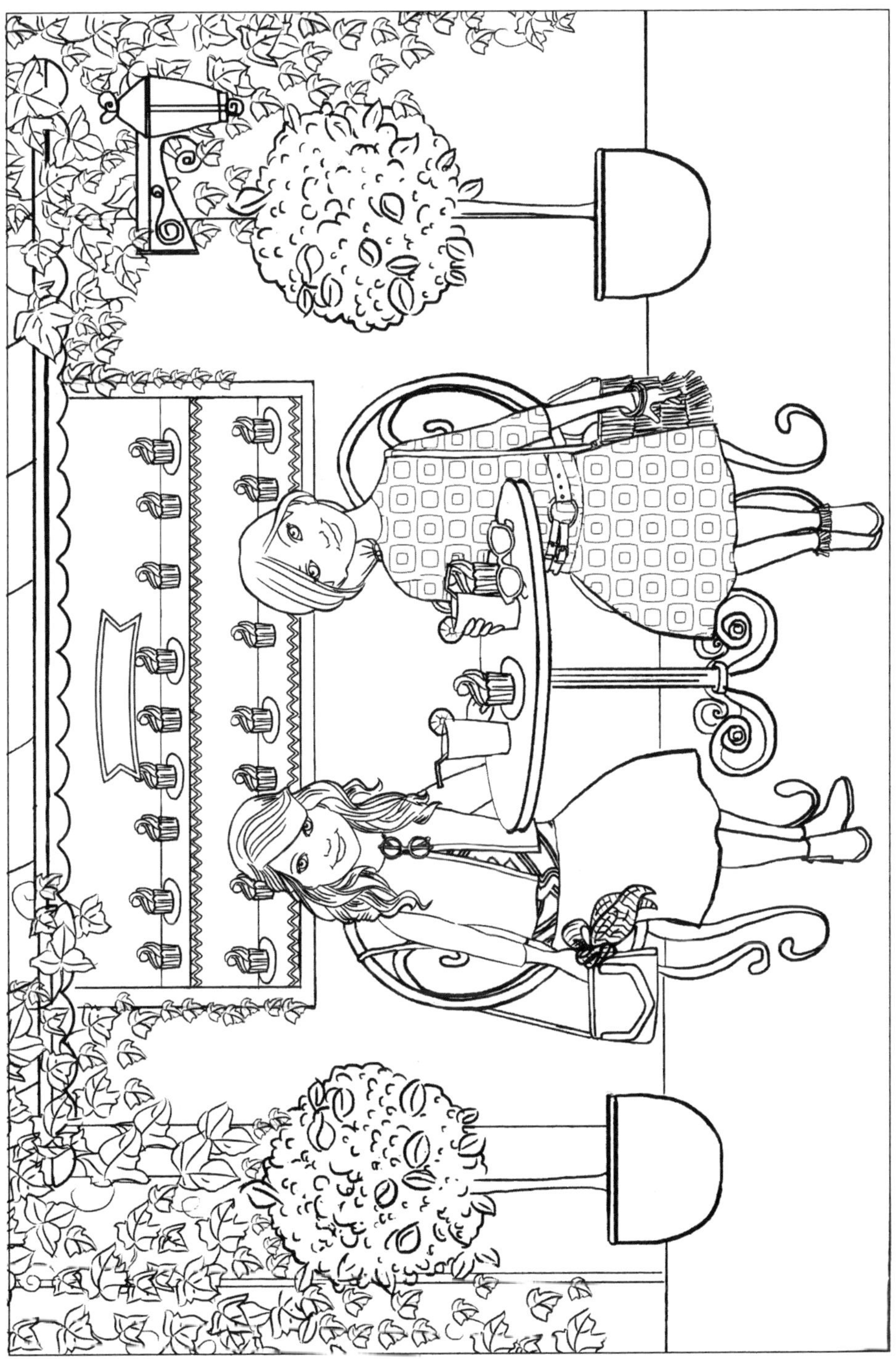

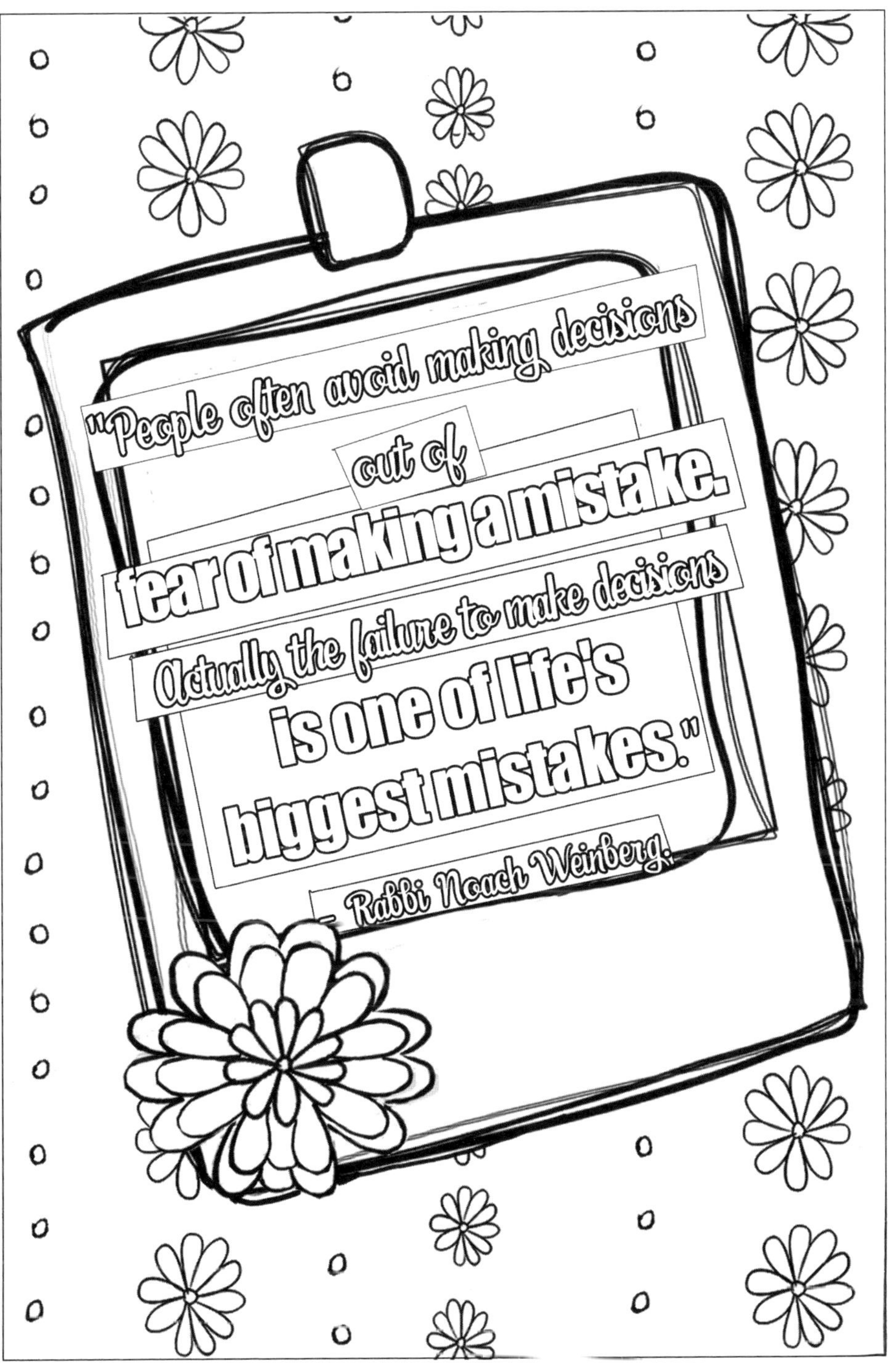
"People often avoid making decisions
out of
fear of making a mistake.
Actually the failure to make decisions
is one of life's
biggest mistakes."
– Rabbi Noach Weinberg.

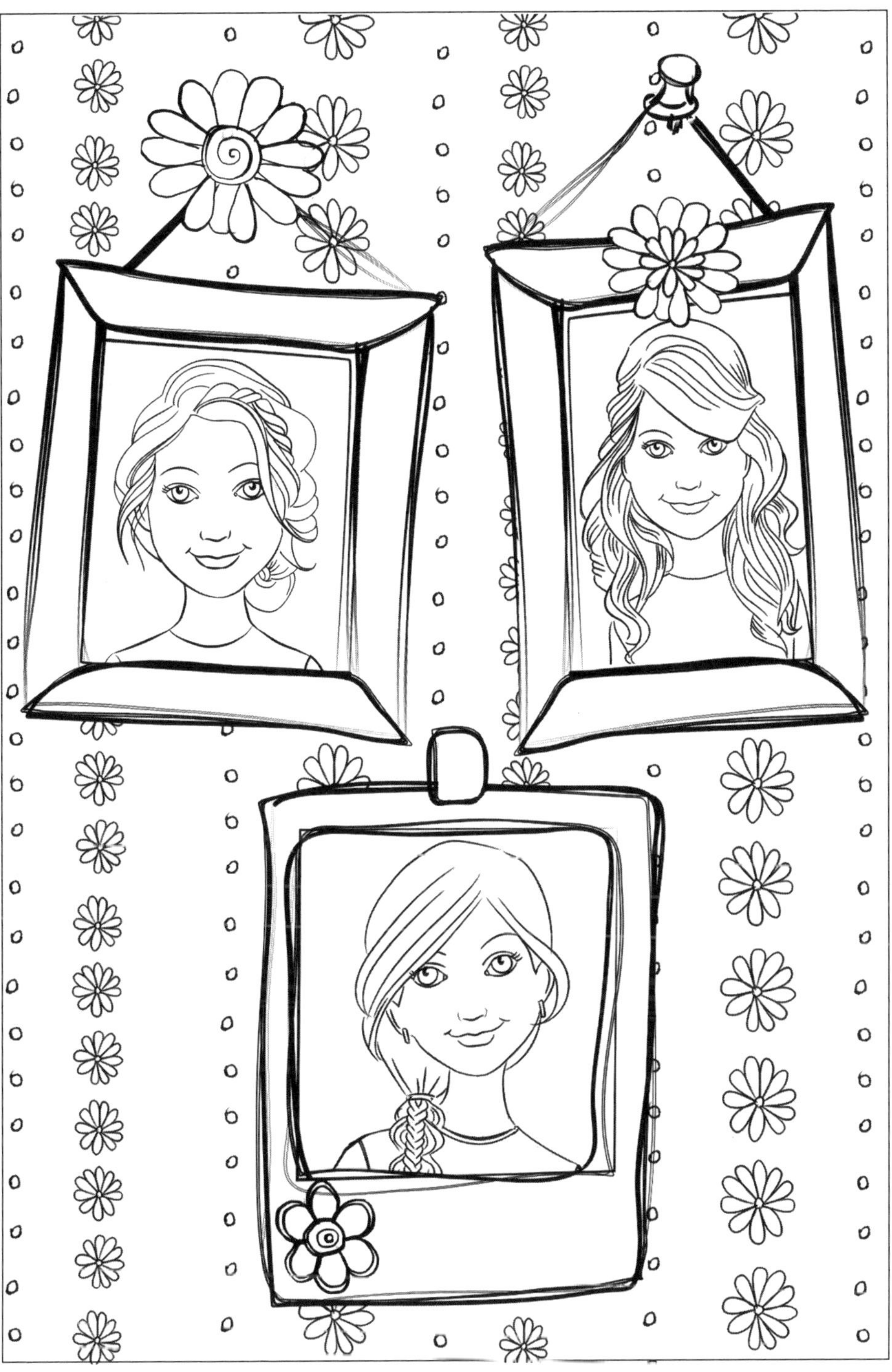

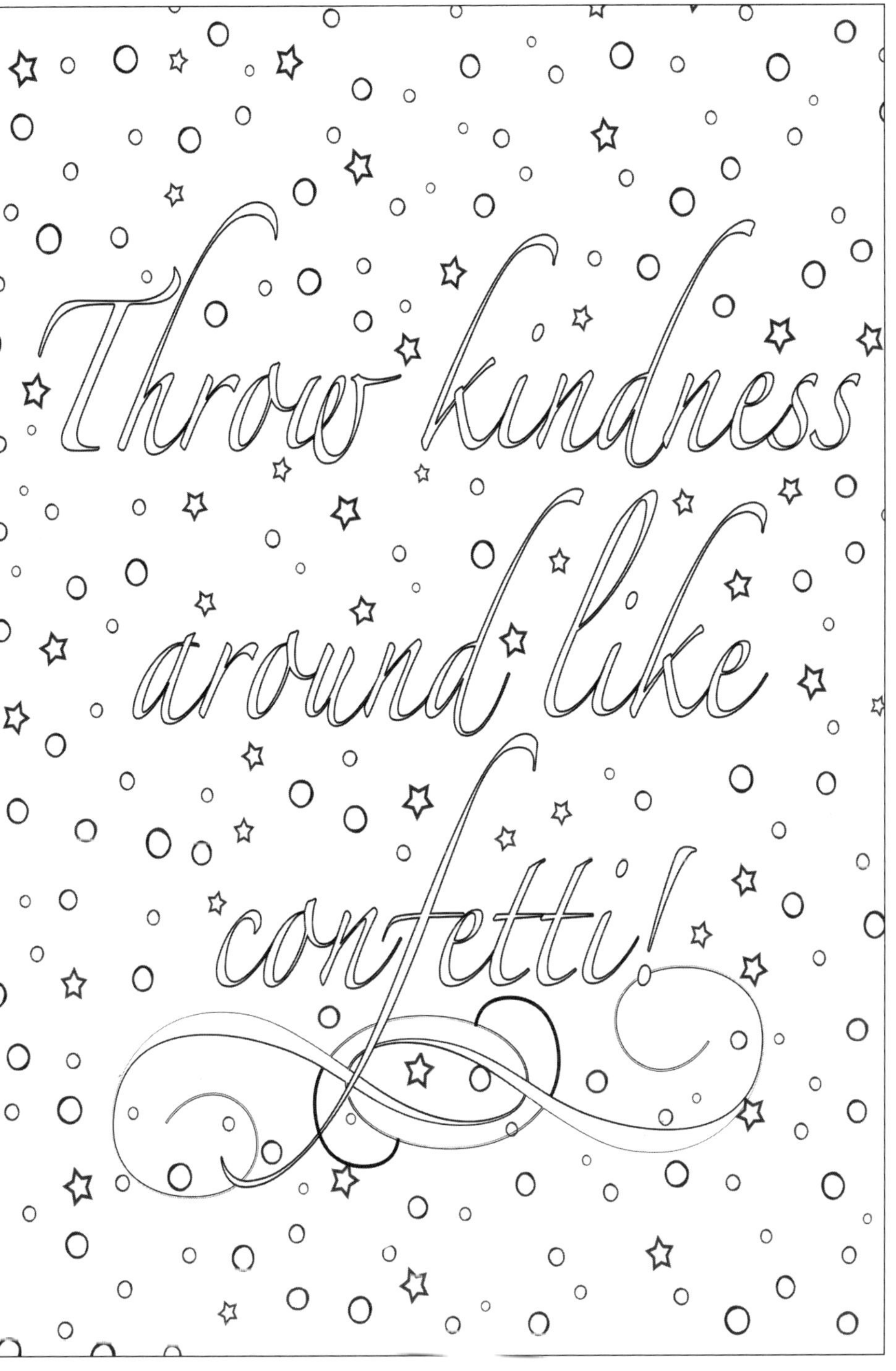
Throw kindness
around like
confetti!

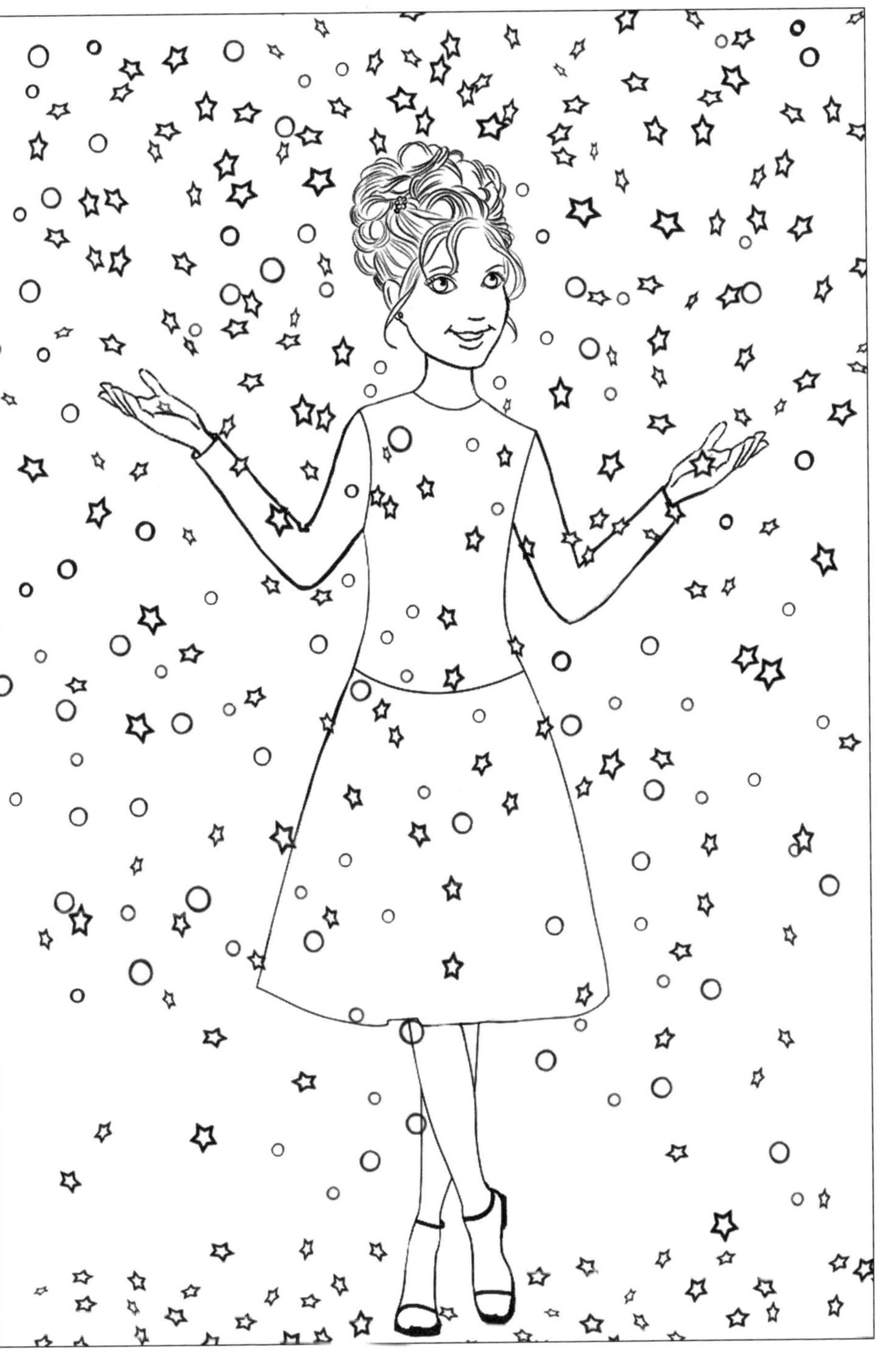

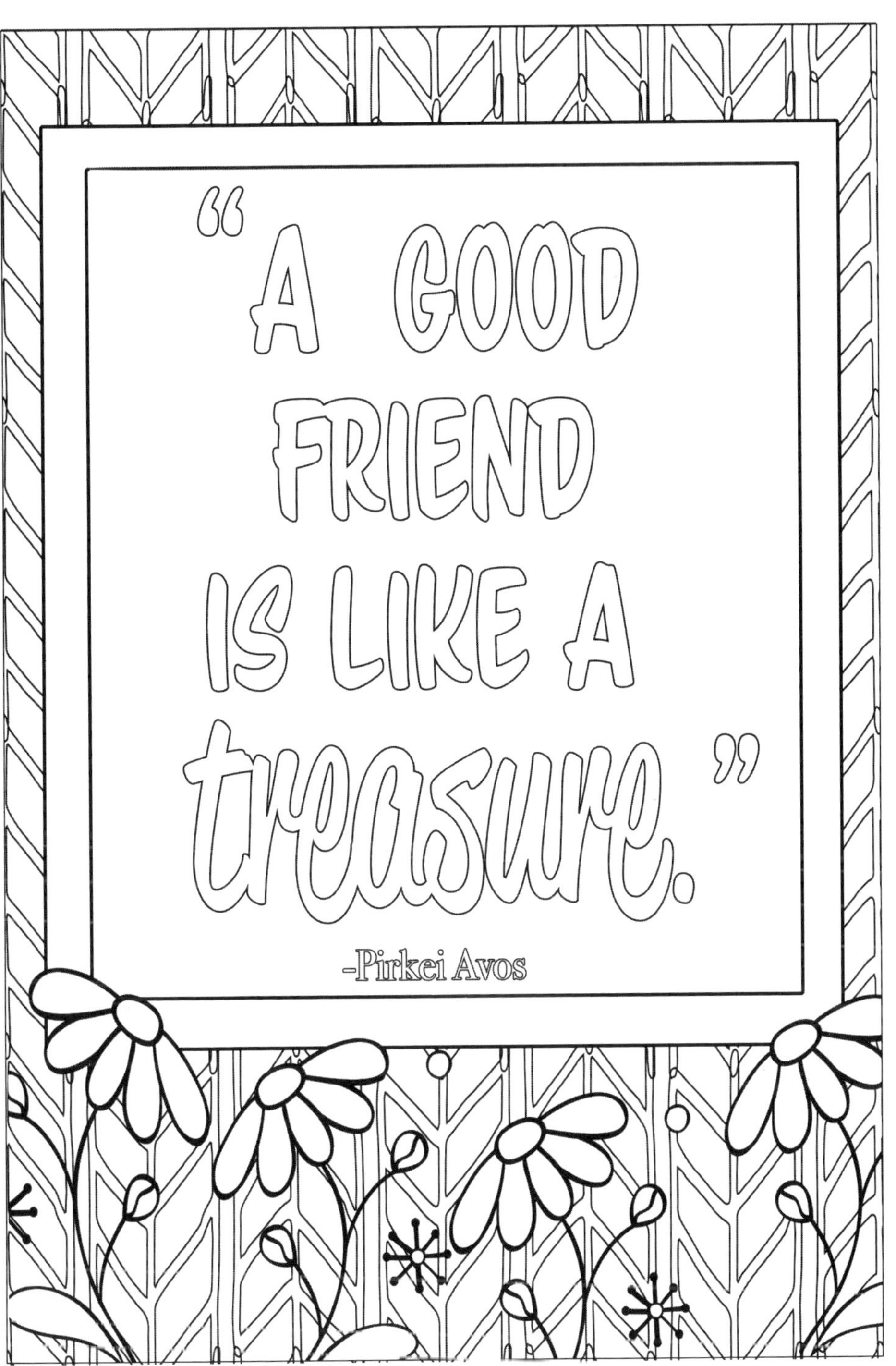
"A GOOD
FRIEND
IS LIKE A
treasure."
-Pirkei Avos

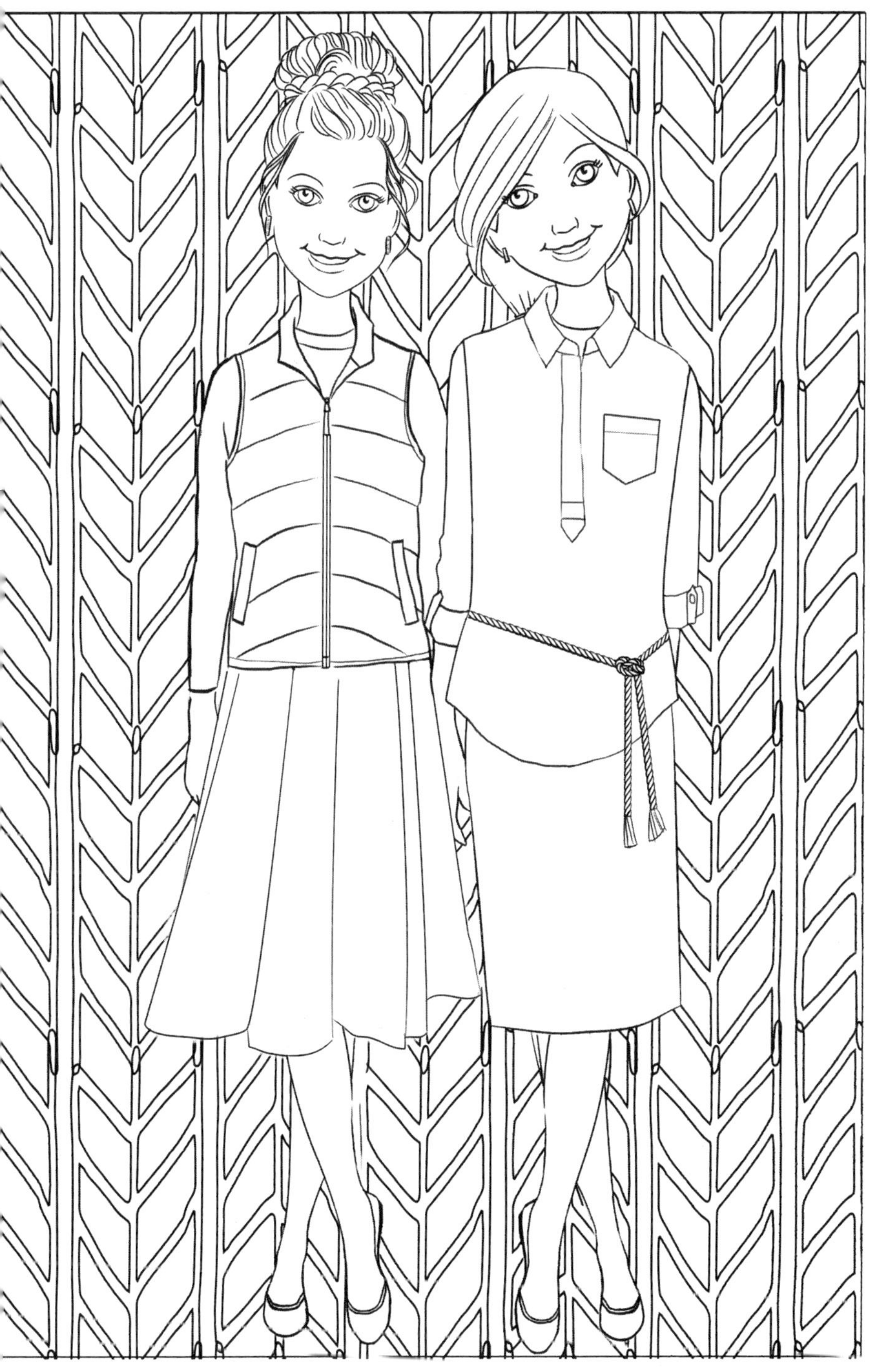

Mosaica Press, Inc.

ISBN-10: 1-946351-23-7 ISBN-13: 978-1-946351-23-4

Published and distributed by Mosaica Press, Inc.
www.mosaicapress.com info@mosaicapress.com

Check out the other sketchbooks in the *Adina* series!

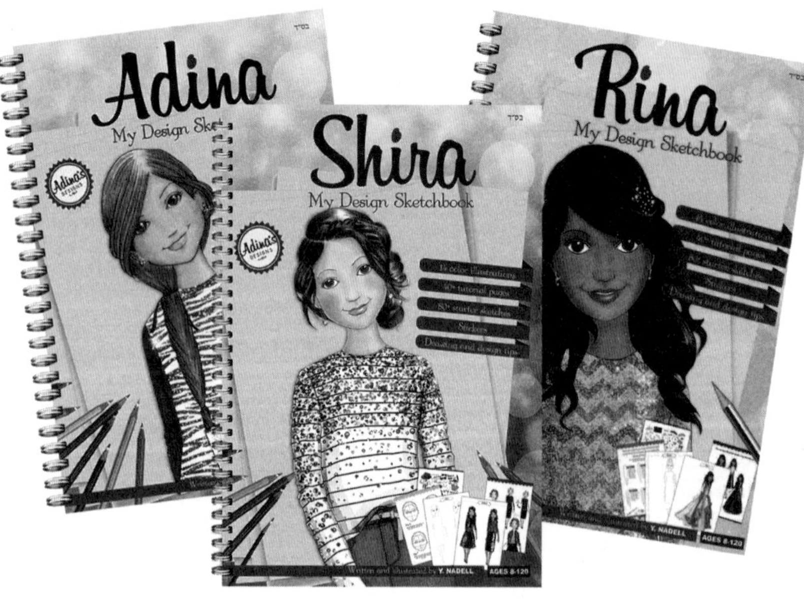

For more information, visit
www.adinasdesigns.com